DISEQUILIBRIUM ECONOMICS

Disequilibrium Economics

J. VAN DOORN

Lecturer in Economics, University of Durham

A HALSTED PRESS BOOK

JOHN WILEY & SONS
New York – Toronto

First published in the United Kingdom 1975 by
The Macmillan Press Ltd

Published in the U.S.A., Canada and Latin America by
Halsted Press, a Division of
John Wiley & Sons, Inc.
New York

Printed in Great Britain

Library of Congress Cataloging in Publication Data

Doorn, Jacques van.
    Disequilibrium economics.

    "A Halsted Press book."
    Bibliography: p.
        1. Equilibrium (Economics)   2. Economic stabilization—
Mathematical models.   I.   Title.
HB145.D66   330'.01'8   75-19139
    ISBN 0 470-89902-6

Contents

Preface and Acknowledgements

This book developed from a course of lectures given over a number of years at the University of Durham and reflects an attempt to introduce the fundamentals of non-stochastic dynamic processes to second- and third-year undergraduates. Such a treatment seems necessary since most undergraduate texts hardly go beyond comparative static analysis.

In this book, therefore, an alternative way of looking at economic phenomena is pursued, and attention is focused principally on adjustment processes resulting from disequilibrium situations, rather than on a comparison of equilibrium situations alone. Most of the analysis is of a short-run nature. Problems of stock-supply determination such as capital accumulation, which may or may not be an equilibrium process in itself, are therefore not explicitly discussed.

Some mathematics is essential for analysing dynamic processes, but since the models which are discussed are put in discrete terms, it has been possible to restrict the use of mathematics to discrete time equations only. Their interpretation and solution is dealt with in an Appendix.

Success or failure of any text depends largely upon feedback from students and colleagues in the earlier stages of writing. In this connection I must express my particular gratitude to Walter Elkan and Richard Morley of the University of Durham and David Pearce of the University of Leicester and George McKenzie of the University of Southampton for many helpful comments; any resulting failure is in no way attributable to them. I would also like to thank Mrs S. Drake for her excellent typing assistance.

J. v. D.

1 Introduction

CONCEPTS

Economic literature is full of confusing terminology. Like Humpty Dumpty, many authors not only wilfully make words mean what they choose them to mean, but they also apply definitions that are not even internally consistent.

This seems particularly true in relation to concepts like 'equilibrium', 'disequilibrium', 'statics' and 'dynamics', concepts that take a central position in this book. Some clarification of what will be meant by these terms here seems almost obligatory.

According to Machlup, an 'equilibrium' is best defined as 'a constellation of selected interrelated variables, so adjusted to one another that no inherent tendency to change prevails in the model which they constitute' ([50] p. 54). Several points in this definition deserve attention.

First, it should be noted that equilibrium is related to a *constellation of interrelated variables*. In other words, equilibrium is a situation related to a particular theory or model. The mere equality of any two variables in a certain period, say quantity demanded and quantity supplied, or equality of the sums of both sides of the balance of payments, does not constitute an equilibrium in the above sense. It just states an accounting identity involving flows or stocks.[1] Quantity demanded and supplied, or the items on the balance of payments, are not purely autonomous, but are related to various other explanatory variables such as prices and incomes or employment and exchange rates, which themselves again depend on other

---

[1] Without any harm we can however follow present practice and refer to these situations as temporary or short-run equilibria.

9

values. An equilibrium only exists within a framework of relationships, which we call a *model*, when *all* dependent variables simultaneously show no endogenous tendency to change.

This brings us to a second point. The word *selected* suggests a freedom to choose any particular theory that is thought to give an adequate explanation of the situation involved. Here a conflict of internal consistency could arise. A large number of competing theories, varying in complexity and in the choice of key variables exists, and it seems easier for the simpler theories to identify an equilibrium situation than for the complex, say a 100-odd equation models to do so. 'Equilibrium' is therefore a conditional concept, it depends on the theory selected by the researcher.

An equilibrium for a particular model, then, is a situation characterised by an absence of an endogenous tendency to change, and the analysis of equilibrium situations is therefore referred to as *static* analysis. The term 'statics' and its opposite, 'dynamics', show such a wide variety of interpretations that Machlup remarked: 'Whenever another more readily understood word or phrase is available in lieu of either statics or dynamics, it should be preferred' ([51] p. 42).

In recent years most economists seem to have accepted the Tinbergen [76]–Frisch [27] suggestion that a theory be denoted 'dynamic' if it involves *variables at different points of time*. This practice is adopted here too. It is not sufficient for a model to be labelled as dynamic if time is explicitly introduced. What should be the case is that not all variables refer to the same time period. It will then be possible to trace out a self-generating – endogenous – time path of development.

Because static models are related to equilibrium positions it does not mean that dynamic models are solely concerned with disequilibrium positions. Dynamic models can generate equilibrium or disequilibrium time paths. The study of behaviour of equilibrium paths of a given model was called by Hahn and Matthews [32] *equilibrium dynamics*. An example is the warranted rate of growth path in the Harrod theory of economic growth. It shows the maximum rate of growth when *ex ante* supply of savings equals its demand. *Disequilibrium*

10

dynamics is concerned with the study of disequilibrium time paths, when one or more of the equilibrium conditions no longer hold. Examples are the various time paths of Cobweb and lagged accelerator models and the knife-edge problem in economic growth. In this book elementary disequilibrium processes will be studied.

How these mechanisms operate has yet to be made clear. However, we may be able to get a good idea of what it is all about by borrowing an example from the theory of servomechanisms. The basic ingredient of such a system is an *error-adjustment* mechanism.

Consider a system consisting of a centrally heated house with a thermostatic heat control. The system is displayed in a block diagram,[1] as in Fig. 1, in which heat flows are shown by con-

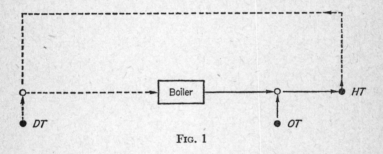

FIG. 1

tinuous lines, their direction by the arrowhead, and the information flow by a broken line. The open circles indicate a differential operation (addition, subtraction) and the solid circles the level of temperature. Three constants or parameters appear in the system, the desired temperature DT, outside temperature OT, and the capacity of the boiler which, when switched on, always works at full speed. The objective of the system is to keep house temperature HT as close as possible to the desired temperature (the equilibrium value for the system),

[1] Block diagrams to illustrate the principle of servo-mechanisms were originally developed by engineers. Goodwin [29] and Phillips [59] were among the first economists to show their relevance to economic systems.

11

to minimise the difference or error. In the initial situation all temperatures are assumed to be equal. The boiler is out. A sudden change in weather lowers the outside temperature and the house temperature will drop consequently. When the difference between desired temperature and house temperature, known as the error, exceeds some critical value (a decision lag), the boiler will start to eliminate the difference (error). It takes time before the water in the system is sufficiently heated to offset the loss of heat to the outside (a production lag) and house temperature may drop slightly further. House temperature will start rising as soon as heat generation exceeds the loss, and will continue until the desired level is reached. The fire is switched off, but for a while the water will continue to supply more heat, so house temperature will rise slightly above desired temperature (overshooting the equilibrium) till a maximum temperature is reached. The temperature will then drop again. Graphically we get a smooth oscillatory movement around the desired temperature level as in Fig. 2.

The structure of this system is called a *closed loop system*. It encompasses a lower loop, the heat flow, and a control loop or feedback loop by means of which house temperature is

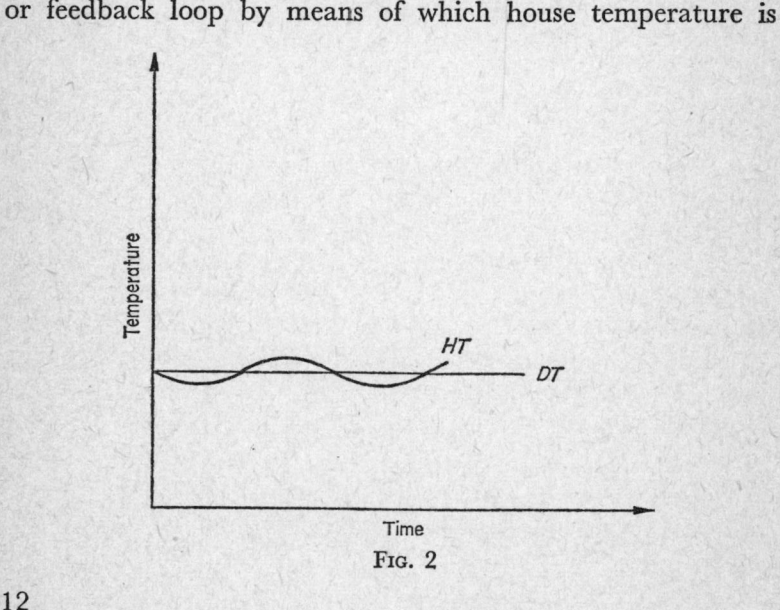

Fig. 2

compared with desired temperature. The measured error is fed back into the system to change the heat flow in such a way as to diminish the difference between the house temperature and the desired level. The feedback is said to be negative.

What this example of a thermostatic control system shows is that disequilibrium systems have a built-in error adjustment mechanism that sets the system in motion. It can bring the system back to an equilibrium value or lead the system farther away from equilibrium in other cases.

We can look at economic disequilibrium processes in the same way. We substitute equilibrium value for desired value, and call the difference in each period between equilibrium and actual values the error. It then depends on economic reactions of the various individuals or macro units to this error whether the system will move closer to equilibrium or not.

Unlike machines, human beings do not react in a passive-mechanistic way once a disequilibrium situation has arisen. Individuals do not base decisions on what is being observed in the market at some point in time alone. They usually have recorded past observations in their memories, and they may even think they know better than the market what future developments will be. In other words, they have anticipations or expectations about the future course of developments and may act on their belief. This will have implications for the error-adjustment process.

House sellers, for instance, when expecting future prices to be higher than present prices, may, being profit maximisers, wish to delay any transactions being made now and withdraw from the market. But this very action reduces market supply thereby speeding up house-price increases most effectively. This could raise expectations even more, supply could be reduced even further, and house prices could rise even faster. Tremendous social problems are created as a result of the accelerated rise in prices if this process is allowed to continue for some time. The losers, in the short run (since such a process is unlikely to last indefinitely), are not the house owners but those who planned to buy a house for the first time, usually those in the lower brackets of the income distribution. An

13

economic policy to deal with these problems cannot solely rely on a static house-market model. Just as it takes time before a super-oiltanker actually changes its course once the rudder has been reset, so it will take time before the house market will respond to policy action. Thus, not only is there a problem that action could come too late, it could also be of insufficient strength to eliminate the disequilibrium process, for instance when it follows an explosive pattern which was not fully recognised when policy decisions were taken. Knowledge of the most likely future development of the market and the time lag of action should therefore be fed back to the policy-makers to make their actions more effective.

Since expectations hypotheses as well as lag structures and their causes take such a central position in dynamic systems we will deal with them first, in the remainder of the chapter, before we turn our attention to a further examination of disequilibrium processes and stabilisation policies.

REASONS FOR LAGS

The error-reduction mechanism which replaces the equilibrium condition in a disequilibrium situation was seen, in our example of a centrally heated house, to be operating through the use of lags.

For the introduction of such a mechanism in an economic context in which the desired or equilibrium value is pursued by actual values, we need lags too.

Lags appear in economic relationships for several reasons, which can be classified as:
(1) technological,
(2) psychological, and
(3) institutional.

The period of time from which production on a good has started, whether it is to grow a crop or to ship an item, until it emerges as a finished good is called the production lag or output lag. It is a technological phenomenon. A change in the level of demand when a production lag exists is not instantaneously met by a change in the level of output, if stocks are

14

absent. Nor need the discrepancy between desired and actual production levels be restored in the following time period or in the periods thereafter. Whether this discrepancy or error will be reduced to zero when an equilibrium level will be approached, or whether it will continue to increase over time depends crucially on the error-adjustment mechanism. In other words, the development through time depends on producers' and demanders' reactions and the structure of the output lag.

The actual length of the production lag varies as a result of employing different technological processes. Metzler [53], compared various lags and stressed the importance of what he called the Lundberg lag (production lag) for the analysis of business-cycle theory. He found an average lag of four quarters for the period from 1921 to 1930. A much shorter delay was found by Carlson [12] in a recent study. He estimated the average production period for two-digit U.S. manufacturing industries at less than a quarter, and found an increasing dispersion between estimates of production periods at lower levels of aggregation.

Psychological inertia and expectations are other reasons for lags to appear in behavioural relationships. Households and firms may not adjust instantaneously to changed conditions due to the memory of past conditions or because new conditions were not anticipated in time. If, say, households receive an increase in income, they will eventually spend some fraction of it. However, they may not do so immediately if their spending behaviour is governed by the level of income that they received in the past and which they continue to regard as their 'normal' income. Suppose the relevant spending hypothesis is fairly accurately represented by a proportional consumption function with a one period delay (often called a Robertsonian lag [63]) written as

$$C_t = a_1 Y_{t-1} \tag{1.1}$$

Since time is treated as a discrete variable, an income change between two successive periods is defined as

$$\Delta Y_t = Y_t - Y_{t-1} \tag{1.2}$$

15

Using this expression, we can rewrite equation (1.1) as

$$C_t = a_1 Y_t - a_1 \Delta Y_t \qquad (1.3)$$

which tells us that, despite the increase in income, the level of spending remains unchanged.

A Robertsonian lag has important methodological advantages when used to explain the Keynesian investment multiplier. It is surely too simple a device to predict savings or consumption expenditures. More sophisticated *habit persistence* hypotheses were formulated, to improve the predictive performance of the consumption function, by Duesenberry [19], Modigliani [54], Brown [8] and Friedman [22], with current consumption being related to past income or consumption levels, peak levels, or even the stock of wealth. Lag structures consequently became more complex too.

So far both terms, inertia and expectations, have been used more or less indiscriminately. There is a difference in meaning, however. Inertia refers to a slowness in response. Habits and customs may reduce sensitivity to new conditions, and a behavioural lag results. With expectations things are the other way around. Present behaviour is adjusted to anticipated future events. A profit-maximising entrepreneur, for instance, makes his investment decisions on what he expects to earn in the near future. He does not know the future any better than does a professional forecaster, and both will use historical values to give information about expected values. Both psychological inertia and expectations are quantified through the use of lags. Their operational difference therefore seems questionable.

The use of lagged relationships is certainly not restricted to the analysis of consumer behaviour alone. Expectational variables play an important role in almost every part of economic analysis, particularly in investment demand and monetary theory.

Sometimes the reason why adjustments only take place after a lapse of time is that the laws and institutions of a country rule out an immediate adjustment. For instance, trade contracts have a time clause specified, salaries are paid at regular weekly or monthly intervals, mortgages are repaid over fixed periods, and taxation proposals need parliamentary approval before being implemented. A change in the circular flow of income will therefore not affect all households, all firms, and the government at the same time and to the same extent. When measured at relatively short intervals, say months, a distributed pattern of reactions is the likely outcome in the aggregate. Institutional delays of this kind are not as such very interesting from an economic point of view. What is important and most interesting is to find the time it takes before changes in government policy eventually make themselves felt in, say, the level of employment or the rate of new investment. We shall return to this point, the time lag of fiscal and monetary policy, in Chapter 4.

LAG STRUCTURES

One needs to know two things before a dynamic model can be constructed: first, *why* lags can occur, and this we have discussed; second, *what* structure of lags is implied by a given set of technological, psychological or other conditions, and this will be dealt with now. Three lag structures have found a wide range of applications: first-order, second-order and distributed lags. Both first-order and second-order lags are special cases of the more general distributed lag form.

We have a distributed lag structure when a dependent variable Y, at some time t, is affected by several consecutive values of an independent variable X, at preceding points in time. Algebraically

$$Y_t = a_0 X_t + a_1 X_{t-1} + a_2 X_{t-2} + \ldots \qquad (1.4)$$

where the a_i's have a finite sum and have all the same sign. Under these conditions we can rewrite equation (1.4) into a form with relative, but unspecified, weights such as

$$Y_t = a(\omega_0 X_t + \omega_1 X_{t-1} + \omega_2 X_{t-2} + \ldots), \qquad (1.5)$$

where $\Sigma \omega_i = 1$, $\Sigma a_i = a$, $\omega_i = a_i/a$ and $i = 0, 1, 2, \ldots, \infty$.

The time form of the lags is indicated by the set of coefficients

a_0, a_1, a_2,... Thus, a first-order lag form is derived from equation (1.5) when all a_i's apart from a_1 are set equal to zero. Hence

$$Y_t = a(\omega_1)X_{t-1} \qquad (1.6)$$

where $\omega_1 = 1$. This equation tells us that a change in the level of X has its full impact on Y exactly one period later. Earlier values of Y or later values are completely unaffected.

Another lag structure that regularly appears in dynamic models, the second-order lag, is derived in the same way. Thus,

$$Y_t = a(\omega_1 X_{t-1} + \omega_2 X_{t-2})$$

but since $\omega_1 + \omega_2 = 1$

$$Y_t = a(1 - \omega_2)X_{t-1} + a(\omega_2)X_{t-2} \qquad (1.7)$$

It is postulated in equation (1.7) that Y_t is related to discrete values of X, lagged one and two periods respectively. Without further information (remember that we are using unspecified weights) it is impossible to say whether the peak response is brought about by changes in period $t-1$ or $t-2$. It is obvious that this gap should be filled by any particular theory that postulates the use of a relation like equation (1.7).

Models involving first- or second-order lags should be treated with care. They explicitly exclude any possible response that may come from periods other than those specified. This may not be unrealistic when individual behaviour is studied and when time periods are relatively long. On the other hand, when aggregate behaviour is analysed, it has to be realised that the impact of a changed condition need not reach all individuals at the same time because of technical and institutional delays, and that individuals differ in their speed of response. The use of a distributed lag structure seems to be more relevant in these cases, since total response is likely to be spread over several periods.

This however creates a number of problems. Consider again equation (1.4)

$$Y_t = a_0 X_t + a_1 X_{t-1} + a_2 X_{t-2} + \ldots$$

In principle there can be any number of a_i's, and thus a question of efficiency arises when large numbers of observations are available. One approach is to maximise explanation, by adding more historical values, in terms of the coefficient of determination R^2 with the size of the standard errors for the regression coefficient has side constraints. This is one way of arriving at an 'optimal' lag structure. For more sophisticated methods of finding optimum lag structures see De Leeuw [16] and Almon [3]. Another problem concerns the parameters. Since no theory predicts equality of all a_i's, the question arises as to what other relationship, if any, may exist between them. A third problem is statistical. Estimated values for a_i's are inaccurate due to strong multi-collinearity between the explanatory variables.

These problems have been generally acknowledged and various ways have been suggested to meet them. A most useful lag specification was suggested by Koyck [46] in his analysis of investment behaviour. He related the size of the capital stock not to the previous output level, as in the naïve accelerator theory, but to different output values in the past. The influence of these variables was assumed to decline geometrically with the order of the lag.

Instead of using the unspecified relative weights, the Koyck hypothesis asserts

$$\omega_i = (1 - \lambda)\lambda^i \quad \text{assuming} \mid \lambda \mid \leqslant 1.$$

Substitution into equation (1.5) gives

$$Y_t = a[(1 - \lambda)(X_t + \lambda X_{t-1} + \lambda^2 X_{t-2} + \ldots)]. \qquad (1.8)$$

A surprising simplification of this form is possible if equation (1.8) is lagged once and multiplied through by λ. We obtain

$$\lambda Y_{t-1} = a[(1 - \lambda)(\lambda X_{t-1} + \lambda^2 X_{t-2} + \lambda^3 X_{t-3} + \ldots)].$$

Subtracting this form from equation (1.8), assuming that beyond the $t-n$ period λ^n will effectively be approaching zero, yields

$$Y_t = \lambda Y_{t-1} + a(1 - \lambda)X_t \qquad (1.9)$$

19

This operation is known in the literature as the *Koyck transformation*. Equation (1.9) is a two-parameter, λ, a, first-order difference equation in Y, in which $1 - \lambda$ is interpreted as the speed of response of Y_t to values of X. The peak response occurs immediately when geometrically declining weights are assumed; further response fades away rapidly when λ is close to 0. The stability of the adjustment process is illustrated below.

Let

$$Y_1 = \lambda Y_0 + a(1 - \lambda)X_1$$

where $X_1 \neq X_0$ and starting from an initial stationary equilibrium. Then

$$
\begin{aligned}
Y_2 &= \lambda Y_1 + a(1 - \lambda)X_1 \\
    &= \lambda[\lambda Y_0 + a(1 - \lambda)X_1] + a(1 - \lambda)X_1 \\
    &= \lambda^2 Y_0 + a(1 - \lambda)(\lambda + 1)X_1
\end{aligned}
$$

and

$$
\begin{aligned}
Y_3 &= \lambda Y_2 + a(1 - \lambda)X_1 \\
    &= \lambda[\lambda^2 Y_0 + a(1 - \lambda)(\lambda + 1)X_1] + a(1 - \lambda)X_1 \\
    &= \lambda^3 Y_0 + a(1 - \lambda)(\lambda^2 + \lambda + 1)X_1
\end{aligned}
$$

Therefore, by induction

$$Y_n = \lambda^n Y_0 + a(1 - \lambda)(\lambda^{n-1} + \lambda^{n-2} + \ldots + \lambda + 1)X_1$$

Since the second term in parentheses is a geometric series it equals

$$(1 - \lambda^n)/(1 - \lambda).$$

Therefore $Y_n = \lambda^n Y_0 + a(1 - \lambda^n)X_1$. If and only if $0 < \lambda < 1$ will $\lambda^n \to 0$ and will Y converge to an equilibrium $Y_n \to aX_1$. It is obvious that with equation (1.9) a much more manageable form has been obtained compared with equation (1.4).

Although we have shown how various lag structures are formulated and related to each other, an important problem still remains unresolved. When examples of dynamic analysis are consulted it often seems that no theoretical justification is given for a particular lag structure. Whether a one-period lag, a two-period lag, or a special distributed lag reflects the pattern of response best is usually determined on *a priori* grounds. Rarely is it desired as an implication of theoretical reasoning.

What is not denied is that psychological, technological and other conditions are a basis for lagged relationships, but it is argued that it is not always explicitly stated which lag structure is implied, nor does it always become clear which weight distribution should be used.[1] The point made is not just an academic one. As we shall see in further chapters, the choice of a lag structure reflects the error-adjustment mechanism of a disequilibrium model, and therefore its stability.

EXPECTATIONS

In an economic disequilibrium system where on-going processes are analysed some assumption must have been made either explicitly or implicitly on expectations concerning the behaviour of prices and income.

But how do households and firms form their expectations? A number of alternative hypotheses have been formulated and examined which fall broadly into two categories: those which assume an element of learning from past errors and those which do not.

Consider a variable X, for which an expected value X^e is to be formed in the next period. The simplest approach is to assume that households will base their expectations on their knowledge about this variable in the past. The other more sophisticated approach is to assume that households or firms base their expectations not only on their knowledge of historical data, but also on the error made in an earlier forecast of X, which is fed back to the latest expectation.

Two naïve, non-learning, hypotheses have been widely used. The first one predicts extrapolative expectations, that is to say, it predicts the next period's value of X to be the same as its current value. In algebraic form

$$X^e_t = X_{t-1} \tag{1.10}$$

It seems surprisingly trivial, yet remarkable application has been made of the extrapolative-expectations hypothesis in

[1] Lag distributions where the weights first rise, reach a peak value and then fall, are discussed in Griliches [30].

dynamic models. The distinction between *ex ante* and *ex post* values as they appear in dynamic multiplier analysis is based on the assumption that savers and/or investors plan their behaviour on the level of income or sales in the previous period. But this is equivalent to saying that savers' behaviour depends on expected income, such that

$$S_t = (1 - a_1)Y^e_t - a_0 \qquad (1.11)$$

and furthermore that their expectations are assumed to be of an extrapolative nature, say

$$Y^e_t = Y_{t-1} \qquad (1.12)$$

Substituting equation (1.12) into equation (1.11) will then yield

$$S_t = (1 - a_1)Y_{t-1} - a_0 \qquad (1.13)$$

Since expectations are of an extrapolative nature, any actual increase in income in period t was not expected and has no effect on intended savings in period t.

Another expectation hypothesis that we shall, in the absence of an element of learning, also classify as naïve relates the expected value of X to its value in the previous period and the direction of change in the past. Hence

$$X^e_t = X_{t-1} + \beta(X_{t-1} - X_{t-2}) \qquad (1.14)$$

where, for simplicity, it will be assumed that $-1 \leqslant \beta \leqslant +1$. The hypothesis was introduced by Metzler [52] in his inventory cycle model and by Goodwin [28] in a Cobweb model, and shows a much more general behaviour than the first hypothesis. The extrapolative hypothesis is derived from it as a special case when the coefficient of expectations β equals zero. Expectations are then completely independent from the direction and rate of change in X.

The hypothesis predicts on the other hand a given rate of change to continue undiminished when the coefficient of expectations equals unity. Thus

$$X^e_t - X_{t-1} = X_{t-1} - X_{t-2}$$

But households and firms expect changes to be partly $(-1 < \beta < 0)$ or wholly $(\beta = -1)$ reversed to the level of period $t-2$ when β is negative. Again, to give operational significance to the expectations variable in the savings function (1.11), we could just as easily replace equation (1.12) by equation (1.14). Instead of using a savings function, the analysis will be carried out with a consumption function.

Thus, if

$$C_t = a_1 Y^e_t + a_0$$

and if expected income is related to observable values as is suggested in equation (1.14), we obtain, after substitution

$$C_t = a_1 \{ Y_{t-1} + \beta (Y_{t-1} - Y_{t-2}) \} + a_0$$

and, slightly rewritten

$$C_t = a_1 Y_t - a_1 \Delta Y_t + a_1 \beta_1 \Delta Y_{t-1} + a_0 \qquad (1.15)$$

The interpretation of equation (1.15) is more complicated than that of equation (1.3).[1] What it says is that consumption is still positively related to the level of income in the previous period (as before) and to a change in the level of income in period $t-1$, which, as long as $\beta > 0$, is expected to continue. In cases where $\beta < 0$, consumers expect the positive change in income in period $t-1$ to return to the level of income in period $t-2$. Current consumption is then not increased. The increase in the level of income in period t itself is completely unexpected and will thus not affect consumer spending in the same period, while consumers' memory only recalls the previous level of income when $\beta = 0$.

Instead of making expectations operational by relating them to a number of selected past observations, as we have done so far, we could construct a more general expectations hypothesis through the introduction of a distributed lag function. Hence

$$X^e_t = a_1 X_{t-1} + a_2 X_{t-2} + a_3 X_{t-3} + \dots \qquad (1.16)$$

[1] Note that in a $C-Y$ diagram, ΔY_t and ΔY_{t-1} operate as shift parameters.

As pointed out earlier, we have to be more precise to make a distributed lag function of more practical use. The analysis will therefore be confined to those cases where all a_i's are of the same sign (non-negative), and where the weight distribution is geometrically declining, thus

$$a_i = \beta\lambda^{i-1}$$

where $0 < \lambda < 1$ for all i.

Substitution into equation (1.16) gives

$$X^e{}_t = \beta X_{t-1} + \beta\lambda X_{t-2} + \beta\lambda^2 X_{t-3} + \ldots \tag{1.17}$$

Lagging this equation once, multiplying through by λ and subtracting this result from equation (1.17) yields:

$$X^e{}_t - \lambda X^e{}_{t-1} = \beta X_{t-1} \tag{1.18}$$

What is obtained is an expectations hypothesis with two parameters instead of one, which does not seem to be of much use unless we can establish some relationship between the two parameters. Now recall equation (1.17) and assume that all values of X in the past, up to period $t-1$ are equal to the normal equilibrium value $\bar{X}$, then

$$X^e{}_t = (\beta + \beta\lambda + \beta\lambda^2 + \ldots)\bar{X} \tag{1.19}$$

There are no obvious reasons why a household or firm would now expect things to be different from the equilibrium value in period t. Hence

$$X^e{}_t = \bar{X}$$

and

$$dX^e{}_t/d\bar{X} = \beta + \beta\lambda + \beta\lambda^2 + \ldots = 1$$

Multiplying $1 = \beta + \beta\lambda + \beta\lambda^2 + \ldots$ through by λ yields $\lambda = \beta\lambda + \beta\lambda^2 + \beta\lambda^3 + \ldots$. Subtracting this result from the original form, assuming that beyond the $t-n$ period $\beta\lambda^n \to 0$, as $n \to \infty$, gives $1 - \lambda = \beta$. When this result is substituted in equation (1.18), we obtain a form

$$X^e{}_t = X^e{}_{t-1} + \beta(X_{t-1} - X^e{}_{t-1}), \tag{1.20}$$

which is identical to the so-called *adaptive expectations hypothesis*,[1] when $0 \leqslant \beta \leqslant 1$. What it tells us is that a change in expected values equals a proportion of the difference between actual and expected values in the past. The hypothesis thus implies an element of learning on the part of those to whom it applies. The new expectation equals the previous one, when the latter turned out to be correct, when no forecasting error was made. This seems plausible. It assumes people will continue their behaviour as long as it proves to be flawless. A revision for the latest expectation becomes necessary when past expectations remain unfulfilled.

The naïve extrapolative hypothesis is a special case of the adaptive expectations hypothesis when $\beta = 1$. The feedback from past errors is eliminated. In the other extreme case where $\beta = 0$ we get fixed expectations, independent of current changes.

The adaptive expectations hypothesis has been successfully used in a number of econometric studies. The hypothesis was first suggested by Cagan [10] in the analysis of hyperinflationary (disequilibrium) processes. Friedman [22] used it in his study on consumer behaviour, and Solow [70] used it to analyse the possible trade-off between inflation and unemployment.[2]

A different expectations hypothesis was put forward by Hicks [36]. He defined an elasticity of expectations as the ratio of the proportional change in expected future values of X to the proportional change in its current value. Algebraically

$$\frac{\mathrm{d} \log X^{\mathrm{e}}_t}{\mathrm{d} \log X_t} = \beta$$

[1] What we have shown with these manipulations is the equivalence between the adaptive expectations hypothesis and the statement that X^{e}_t is a moving average of all past values of X_t with geometrically declining weights.

[2] The Arrow and Nerlove [4] formulation of the adaptive expectations hypothesis has, for mathematical convenience, been used here.

and, in discrete form so as to facilitate comparison with the other hypotheses

$$\log X^e{}_t = \log X^e{}_{t-1} + \beta(\log X_t - \log X_{t-1}) \qquad (1.21)$$

The hypothesis implies the latest expectations to be made up from knowledge gained in the past, as summarised in the previous expectation, while a correction is applied for the latest change in prices or income not taken into account when the previous expectation was made.

Two pivotal cases are distinguished: one where the elasticity is zero, implying perfectly inelastic expectations with respect to current values; the other where the elasticity equals unity. Expected values must then change in the same direction and proportion as do current values. Thus, if present prices rise by say 10 per cent people expect future prices to rise by exactly the same amount. The literature contains many interesting cases where unit elasticity does not hold. Keynes's liquidity preference theory is one example.

The hypothesis has been advanced that predictions generated by a dynamic econometric model, based on data up to the time of prediction, are a sort of expectations. Muth [56] elaborated this idea in the so-called *rational expectations hypothesis*.

Prediction with such a model could then be compared with those made by individual households or firms. When market performance is analysed within a Cobweb structure, it is found that its predictions have a sign opposite to those of the individual suppliers. This is a result well worth discussing in the next chapter.

RECOMMENDED READING

A useful discussion of the conditions for static equilibrium in the case of both flow and stock markets is given in Bushaw and Clower [9].

A more mathematical approach to some of the questions raised in this chapter is presented in Allen [2], and Simon [68].

Goodwin [29] is most interesting on closed-loop feedback control.

How expectations are dealt with in econometrics is well explained in Klein [45], while Metzler [52] shows some interesting experiments with different lag distributions in simple macro models.

Articles on distributed lag structures are fairly technical. The reader may wish to consult any of: Solow [69], Jorgenson [42], Griliches [30] and Wallis [79], or again Allen [2].

2 Micro-Disequilibrium Economics

INTRODUCTION

Prices and quantities are determined in markets where individuals meet and exchange goods. A market is in equilibrium when the volume of trading remains constant and prices are not forced to change either; in other words, when no one has an incentive to modify his behaviour. There are various reasons why one might expect markets not to be in equilibrium. First, there are general external influences on the economy as a whole affecting all markets to a certain extent: for example, a bad summer, a change in the rate of population growth or some political event. But there are also specific influences for a particular market, such as a change in tastes brought about by a successful advertising campaign, the effects of which may be hardly noticeable in other markets. In the first case, the approach to the explanation of price and quantity changes is one of general analysis. In the second case, when isolated markets are dealt with, partial analysis is applied. This latter approach is followed here, when first one, and then just two interrelated markets are analysed.

What response could be predicted once initial market equilibrium is disturbed? Each market has two 'control' variables, price and quantity. Two stability mechanisms can thus be considered.[1] In the Walrasian mechanism, price responds, with infinite velocity, to disequilibrium situations. The price is raised when excess demand is positive, and

[1] The reader who is unfamiliar with the operation of these mechanisms is referred to Baumol [7].

28

lowered when it is negative. The mechanism assumes negative feedback: it ensures that the pre-trading price will adjust to a level where the market will be cleared in the short run.[1]

The Walrasian static stability concept was generalised by Hicks [36] for general equilibrium purposes, when the effects of a change in the price of one commodity on the prices of all other commodities were considered. Two stability positions are defined. Equilibrium is called *imperfectly stable* if in an economy with $n+1$ commodities n markets are cleared (zero excess demand at equilibrium prices) with either positive or negative excess demand at a price below or above equilibrium level in the $n+1$ market. A general equilibrium position is called *perfectly stable* if all conditions of stability are satisfied.

A second static stability condition is the Marshallian adjustment mechanism, where quantity adjusts to discrepancies between demand price and supply price.

In the case of a negative feedback, quantity will increase when excess demand price is positive, but sellers will lower their output when excess demand price is negative. Both adjustment mechanisms are not necessarily of a deviation counteracting nature. A new equilibrium may not be reached if:

(*a*) price or quantity moves in the wrong direction, due to positive feedback; or

(*b*) price or quantity initially moves in the right direction but 'over-adjusts' without further correction.

Negative feedback, or the static stability conditions of both mechanisms, takes account of the right direction of the adjustment process. Negative feedback is therefore called a necessary condition for stability. Neither the Walrasian nor the Marshallian static stability conditions have anything to say about the speed of response of prices and quantity to a displacement from equilibrium. Both conditions cannot guarantee whether price or quality may not overshoot the equilibrium values thereby creating unstable oscillations. This is a problem of dynamic stability which is more relevant for us.

---

[1] Negative feedback is also called a static stability condition.

An example of a market where both mechanisms operate under negative feedback but where nevertheless amplified deviations or explosive processes are not excluded is the Cobweb model. The model was originally set up to analyse more formally the statistical studies by Hanau [33] on systematic fluctuations in the hog market [75].

It was readily understood that in its simplest form, the Cobweb model could only serve as a rough approximation. Not all students of agricultural economics take the naïve form of the model as being very valid, although successful attempts to analyse the dynamics of an agricultural market have been made using the model [73].

THE COBWEB MODEL

The basic assumptions of the Cobweb model are:

(a) supply depends completely on expected price;
(b) actual market price adjusts to demand, so as to eliminate excess demand instantaneously in the trading period;
(c) expected price equals previous equilibrium price, the length of the delay being determined by the production lag; and
(d) there are no inventories, and neither buyers nor sellers have an incentive to speculate.

Algebraically the model consists of the following set of equations:

$$q^d_t = \alpha_0 - \alpha_1 p_t \tag{2.1}$$
$$q^s_t = \beta_0 + \beta_1 p^e_t \tag{2.2}$$
$$q^d_t = q^s_t \tag{2.3}$$
$$p^e_t = p_{t-1} \tag{2.4}$$

with parametric conditions $\alpha_1 > 0$ and $\beta_1 > 0$.

Quantity demanded q^d_t in period t, depends upon the price p_t in the same period, but quantity supplied q^s_t depends upon the expected market clearing price p^e_t, while equation (2.4) assumes that suppliers expect the market clearing price always to be the same as last period's price. It is furthermore assumed that quantity demanded in period t will always equal quantity supplied in the same period, through variations in the market price.

The model is dynamic since not all variables refer to the same period, and consists of four independent linear equations and five variables. One of these, p_{t-1}, is predetermined.

Substituting equations (2.1), (2.2) and (2.4) into (2.3), reduces the model to a single first-order difference equation

$$p_t = -\frac{\beta_1}{a_1} p_{t-1} + \frac{a_0 - \beta_0}{a_1} \qquad (2.5)$$

The particular solution, setting $p_{t-1} = p_t = \bar{p}$ is

$$\bar{p} = \frac{a_0 - \beta_0}{a_1 - \beta_1} \qquad (2.6)$$

and corresponds with the static, long-run, equilibrium value, where price repeats itself period after period. The homogeneous solution of the model is

$$p_t = \left(-\frac{\beta_1}{a_1} \right)^t A \qquad (2.7)$$

where A is the arbitrary constant.

The definite solution, given the initial condition of $p_t = p_0$, when $t = 0$ is then

$$p_t = (p_0 - \bar{p}) \left(-\frac{\beta_1}{a_1} \right)^t + \bar{p} \qquad (2.8)$$

An error-adjustment process, stabilising or not, will only then start when $p_0 - \bar{p} \neq 0$, when an exogenous disturbance has taken place, say by a parallel shift in the demand curve. Algebraically

$$q^d{}_t = (a_0 + \sigma) - a_1 p_t \qquad (2.9)$$

where σ is a shift parameter. The new static equilibrium price is therefore

$$\bar{p}_1 = \frac{(a_0 + \sigma) - \beta_0}{a_1 + \beta_1} \qquad (2.10)$$

and equation (2.8) becomes

$$p_t = (p_0 - \bar{p}_1) \left(-\frac{\beta_1}{a_1} \right)^t + \bar{p}_1 \qquad (2.11)$$

31

The time path of the market price is determined by the difference between the initial p_0 and the new $\bar{p}_1$ equilibrium price, multiplied by $\{-(\beta_1/a_1)\}^t$, which, since both β_1 and a_1 are positive, will alternate between positive and negative values from period to period.

The adjustment process is stabilising when the difference between $\bar{p}_1$ and p_t is reduced in subsequent periods: the error is eliminated.[1] This will happen when $|\beta_1/a_1| < 1$. The error will increase over time when $|\beta_1/a_1| > 1$, such that the time path is explosive.

Traditionally, price is measured on the vertical axis and quantity on the horizontal one, the slope of the demand curve is therefore not $-a_1$, but $-(1/a_1)$, and the slope of the supply curve $+(1/\beta_1)$. A market where the demand curve has a steeper slope than the supply curve will thus be unstable. The numerical value of the slope of the demand curve is greater than the numerical value of the slope of the supply curve.

The adjustment process of a stable Cobweb model is visualised in Fig. 3(a), where the S curve represents the unlagged supply equation and the D_0, D_1 curves the demand functions. Initial equilibrium E_0, is disturbed by a shift σ in the demand curve in period $t+1$. No seller expected the price in period $t+1$ to change from its previous equilibrium level in period t. No seller will therefore attempt to sell more than he did in the previous situation. Quantity supplied in period $t+1$ is fixed and independent from market price in $t+1$. This situation is represented by the vertical, short-run supply curve s_1, where $q^s_{t+1} = q_0$, but it also shows a situation of excess demand. This will push prices up, until excess demand is eliminated at a price level where demand matches available supply, that is, where the s_1 curve intersects the demand curve D_1 at point E^1 which is a short-run equilibrium position. The naïve

[1] Note that the difference between prices in subsequent periods is denoted as 'the error'. The intertemporal adjustment process originates from the supply side of the model, where a one-period lag is postulated.

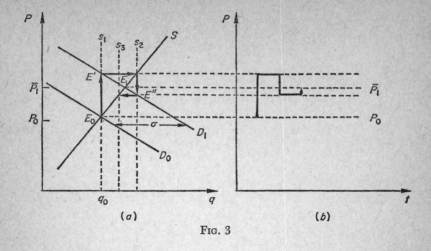

FIG. 3

assumption imposed upon the sellers will make them think that the same high price level will remain in period $t+2$. Quantity supplied is increased to a level where sellers may have maximised their returns if their expectations had been borne out. The short-run supply curve shifts from s_1 to s_2. There is now excess supply in the market and the market price will fall until all that is supplied is absorbed again, which happens at point E^{11}, where the s_2 and D_1 curves intersect. The market is cleared but only temporarily so, because sellers, remembering past price only, will adjust output for the next trading period, and disillusioned as they are, will offer less, consequently prices will rise. This process could continue, with ever decreasing deviations. Prices and quantities in subsequent periods can be traced out repeating the above reasoning, simply by following the arrowheads, thereby weaving a cobweb around the new equilibrium E_1. At that point price will repeat itself, period after period.

The time path of price adjustment is seen in Fig. 3(b). It will be left to the reader to trace out the time path for q_t. Comparing both will show how they move in opposite directions. This phenomenon is the result of the postulated error-adjustment mechanism on the supply side of the market.

33

An explosive Cobweb model, due to over-adjustments by sellers and buyers, is depicted in Fig. 4 (*a*) and (*b*). It could become clear now why different conclusions may be reached by static and dynamic analysis.

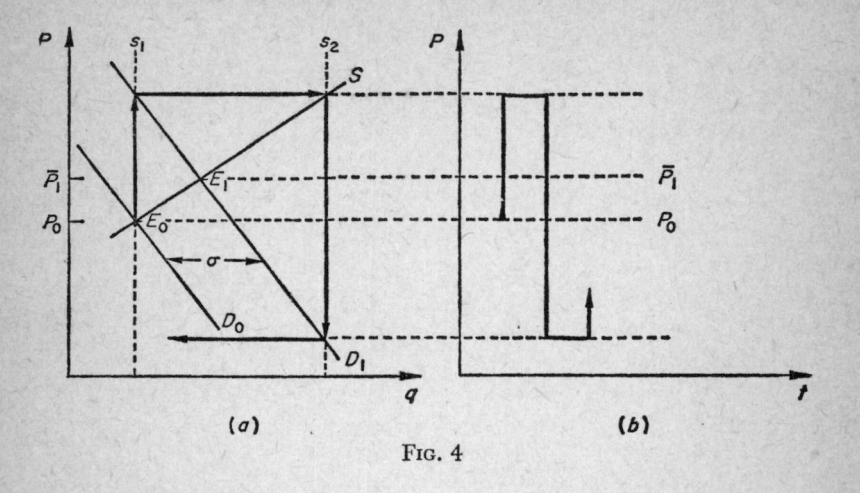

Fig. 4

Static analysis would, because of a shift in the demand curve, have predicted a higher equilibrium price and a higher equilibrium quantity traded, as if negative feedback was a sufficient condition for stability. It is taken for granted that the adjustment will end up at point E_1. Dynamic analysis on the other hand shows in our case an increasing error. In each period the actual market price will move further and further away from the static equilibrium position. Yet, the price will always fall when the actual market price was in excess of the static equilibrium price in the previous period, and will always rise when the market price was below the static equilibrium price. The feedback is clearly negative, but the strength of the adjustment process is too strong. The target value is overshot in each period.

Once an equilibrium is disturbed, the market will never move to a new equilibrium again. The possibility of unstable equilibria is of considerable importance, since it implies

34

that results from static analysis can be seriously misleading. Conclusions about changes in long-run equilibrium values of economic variables will have no predictive power if the model is dynamically unstable. This point was developed by Samuelson [66], who stated 'in order for comparative static analysis to yield fruitful results, we must first develop a theory of dynamics' ([66] pp. 262–3).

So far it has been assumed that quantity supplied and demanded were affected by the price of one good only. Cross effects with other markets are neglected. For certain goods, this procedure seems hard to defend. An increase in the price of lamb may lead to an increase in demand for beef, but it will also affect the prices of goods for which lamb is an important input. This again will affect prices of other goods in other markets and so on and so forth. We can classify three kinds of interrelationships:

(1) horizontal linkages between markets, due to the existence of substitutes and complementary goods;
(2) vertical linkages, where one good is an input into the production of another one, see, for example, the column of an input–output table; and
(3) income linkages, higher prices for a particular good leads to income redistribution affecting the purchase of all goods with non-zero income elasticities.

Full allowances for market interrelationships is given in general (equilibrium) analysis. Here only a simple form of inter-relationship will be studied: the corn–hog cycle.

A CORN–HOG CYCLE[1]

Let the market for hogs be formalised by

$$q^d_{1t} = a_0 - a_1 p_{1t} \qquad (2.12)$$
$$q^s_{1t} = \beta_0 + \beta_1 p_{1t-1} - \beta_2 p_{2t-1} \qquad (2.13)$$
$$q^d_{1t} = q^s_{1t} \qquad (2.14)$$

with parametric conditions, a_1, β_1, $\beta_2 > 0$.

[1] For a different approach see [34].

The demand for good (1), hogs, is determined by their price in the same period. The supply of hogs depends on the price of hogs, and the price of corn, both lagged one period, thereby reflecting naïve expectations. The price of corn is a shift variable for the supply curve. An increase in corn prices shifts the supply curve to the left; at each price fewer hogs will be supplied. The corn market is described by the following set of equations:

$$q^{d}_{2t} = \gamma q^{s}_{1t} \tag{2.15}$$
$$q^{s}_{2t} = \delta_0 + \delta_2 p_{2t-1} \tag{2.16}$$
$$q^{s}_{2t} = q^{d}_{2t} \tag{2.17}$$

with parametric conditions, $\delta_2 > 0$ and $0 < \gamma \leqslant 1$.

The demand function for corn, equation (2.15), is derived from a linear input–output relationship; γ measures the amount of corn needed to 'produce' hogmeat. It is furthermore assumed that corn farmers have extrapolative expectations.

In both markets the error-adjustment mechanism is taken on the supply side. Together they comprise a system of six independent linear equations with seven variables. Two links between both markets are postulated. The first relates the effect of corn prices on the supply of hogs, equation (2.13), the second link is between the demand for hogs and the supply of corn, equation (2.15).

To facilitate interpretation of the interaction of both markets, the static versions of the models are solved first. The reduced form equation for the hog market is obtained by substituting equations (2.12) and (2.13) into (2.14) and solving for p_1, *ceteris paribus* in the corn market. Thus we obtain

$$p_1 = \frac{a_0 - \beta_0}{a_1 + \beta_1} + \frac{\beta_2}{a_1 + \beta_1} p_2 \tag{2.18}$$

The reduced form for p_2 is obtained in a similar way

$$p_2 = \frac{\gamma\beta_0 - \delta_0}{\delta_2 + \gamma\beta_2} + \frac{\gamma\beta_1}{\delta_2 + \gamma\beta_2} p_1 \tag{2.19}$$

ceteris paribus in the hog market.

With two equations (2.18) and (2.19), and two variables,

the static equilibrium values for p_1 and p_2 are uniquely determined, as shown in Fig. 5, where both lines intersect. It is not known however whether this equilibrium is stable or not.

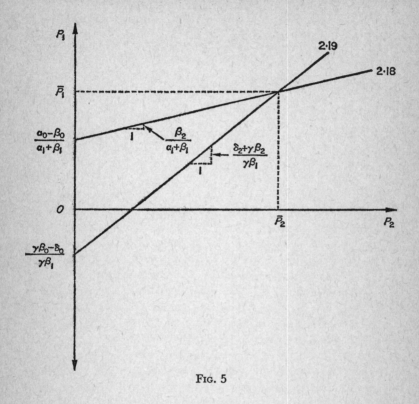

Fig. 5

Only dynamic analysis can answer this question, which we will now do. Solving the dynamic hog market for p_2 gives

$$p_{2t-1} = \frac{\beta_0 - \alpha_0}{\beta_2} + \frac{\beta_1}{\beta_2} p_{1t-1} + \frac{\alpha_1}{\beta_2} p_{1t} \qquad (2.20)$$

and the same procedure for the corn market

$$p_{2t-1} = \frac{\gamma\beta_0 - \delta_0}{\delta_2 + \gamma\beta_2} + \frac{\gamma\beta_1}{\delta_2 + \gamma\beta_2} p_{1t-1} \qquad (2.21)$$

37

Eliminating p_{2t-1} then gives a first-order difference equation in p_1

$$p_{1t} = -\frac{\beta_2}{a_1}\left(\frac{\beta_1}{\beta_2} - \frac{\gamma\beta_1}{\delta_2 + \gamma\beta_2}\right)p_{1t-1} + A$$

where

$$A = -\frac{\gamma\beta_0 + \delta_0}{\delta_2 + \gamma\beta_2} + \frac{\beta_0 - a_0}{\beta_2}$$

For stability it is required that[1]

$$\left|-\frac{\beta_2}{a_1}\left(\frac{\beta_1}{\beta_2} - \frac{\gamma\beta_1}{\delta_2 + \gamma\beta_2}\right)\right| < 1$$

or

$$\left|\frac{\delta_2 + \gamma\beta_2}{\gamma\beta_1}\right| > \left|\frac{\beta_2}{a_1 + \beta_1}\right| \tag{2.22}$$

Equilibrium is thus stable, as long as the numerical value of the slope of equation (2.19) is greater than the numerical value of the slope of equation (2.18), in other words, as long as line (2.19) intersects (2.18) from below. Both markets move towards a final equilibrium once the original one is disturbed. Note that if line (2.19) had intersected (2.18) from above, static analysis would still have predicted an equilibrium. Dynamic analysis would have detected the impossibility of its existence, once an adjustment process had started.

The stability condition for the hog market alone is $|\beta_1/a_1| < 1$ and the stability condition for the corn market is $|\delta_2/\gamma\beta_2| < 1$. How do both conditions relate to the stability condition for the two interrelated markets? Is stability in one market sufficient for the whole system to be stable, or does each market separately have to be stable? This we will now investigate. The stability condition for the two interrelated markets is

$$-1 < -\frac{\beta_2}{a_1}\cdot\frac{\beta_1}{\beta_2} + \frac{\beta_2}{a_1}\cdot\frac{\gamma\beta_1}{\delta_2 + \gamma\beta_2} < +1 \tag{2.23}$$

The right-hand side of the inequality holds if

[1] See Appendix.

38

$$\frac{\beta_1}{a_1} > -\{1 + 1/(\delta_2/\gamma\beta_2)\} \tag{2.24}$$

and the left-hand side if

$$\frac{\beta_1}{a_1} < 1 + 1/(\delta_2/\gamma\beta_2) \tag{2.25}$$

The field of different but positive values for β_1/a_1 and $\delta_2/\gamma\beta_2$ can be divided into two regions, using an equality sign in (2.25) to calculate the boundary, as in Fig. 6. The hatched

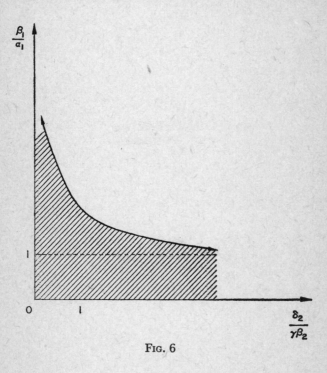

FIG. 6

region shows all stable combinations. It turns out that even if both markets are unstable separately, together they can still be stable. There is nothing wrong with this conclusion. Just remember that the price of hogs acts as a shift parameter in the corn market and so does the price of corn in the hog market.

To give an example: an increase in the demand for hogs in period t will raise the price and more (too much) will be supplied in the next period $(t+1)$. The increased demand for hogs will also increase the demand for corn, thus corn prices will rise too. But the increased corn price could reduce the supply for hogs in $(t+1)$ such that excess supply (as a result of naïve expectations) is to some extent eliminated. Hog prices will therefore not decrease as strongly as could have been the case in a partial analysis. Shifts in supply and demand functions will therefore, under certain conditions, offset an explosive movement in either one or both markets. So far interactions between only two markets were studied. If preferred, the reader can extend the analysis including more linkages, but the mathematics become rather complicated. For an example see Goodwin [28], and Arrow and Nerlove [4].

A COBWEB MODEL WITH LEARNING

It has been argued that instability in particular markets could be the result of the way in which transactors form their expectations. It is therefore most tempting to try to analyse how different expectations affect the conditions for market stability. Goodwin [28] experimented with a hypothesis in which expected prices were related to previous prices and their latest rate of change. As we explained earlier, no element of learning was involved in this process. Nerlove [57] analysed a Cobweb model in which the adaptive expectations hypothesis had replaced the extrapolative expectations hypothesis. The model he used consisted of the equations

$$q^d{}_t = \alpha_0 - \alpha_1 p_t \qquad (2.26)$$
$$q^s{}_t = \beta_0 + \beta_1 p^e{}_t \qquad (2.27)$$
$$q^d{}_t = q^s{}_t \qquad (2.28)$$
$$p^e{}_t = p^e{}_{t-1} + \epsilon(p_{t-1} - p^e{}_{t-1}) \qquad (2.29)$$

with parametric conditions $\alpha_1, \beta_1 > 0$ and $0 < \epsilon \leqslant 1$.

Rewriting the supply equation (2.27) as a function of $p^e{}_t$, lagging it once and substituting the lagged and unlagged forms into (2.29), gives

$$q^s{}_t = (1-\epsilon)q^s{}_{t-1} + \beta_1\epsilon p_{t-1} + \epsilon\beta_0 \tag{2.30}$$

Short-run equilibrium is defined by equation (2.28), which holds for every period, hence

$$q^d{}_t = q^s{}_t \quad \text{and} \quad q^d{}_{t-1} = q^s{}_{t-1}, \quad \text{etc.}$$

In equation (2.30), the $q^s{}_t$ and $q^s{}_{t-1}$ terms are now eliminated by substitution of the lagged and unlagged demand equation, hence

$$a_0 - a_1 p_t = (1-\epsilon)(a_0 - a_1 p_{t-1}) + \beta_1\epsilon p_{t-1} + \epsilon\beta_0$$

or

$$p_t = \left\{1 - \epsilon\left(1 + \frac{\beta_1}{a_1}\right)\right\} p_{t-1} + \epsilon\left(\frac{a_0 - \beta_0}{a_1}\right) \tag{2.31}$$

which is a first-order difference equation in p. The particular solution is

$$\bar{p} = \frac{a_0 - \beta_0}{a_1 + \beta_1} \tag{2.32}$$

which is identical to the long-run equilibrium price of the naïve static model. The definite solution, given $p_t = p_0$ when $t = 0$ is

$$p_t = (p_0 - \bar{p})\left\{1 - \epsilon\left(1 + \frac{\beta_1}{a_1}\right)\right\}^t + \bar{p} \tag{2.33}$$

and describes the time path of deviations around the long-run equilibrium value $\bar{p}$, as $\bar{p} \neq p_0$

A necessary and sufficient condition for stability is

$$\left| 1 - \epsilon\left(1 + \frac{\beta_1}{a_1}\right) \right| < 1 \tag{2.34}$$

and rearranged

$$1 - < \frac{\beta_1}{a_1} < \frac{2}{\epsilon} - 1 \tag{2.35}$$

In the extreme case of extrapolative expectations $\epsilon = 1$ and the inequality reduces to the naïve Cobweb stability condition.

For values of $0 < \epsilon < 1$, the right-hand side of the inequality will increase, implying that, even if $\beta_1/a_1 > 1$, market stability is still possible. The smaller ϵ, i.e. the smaller the weight people give to p_{t-1}, the more stable the market could become. This seems to conform to the earlier statement that extrapolative expectations tend to destabilise markets. Thus, if ways can be found to influence expectations, unstable markets are likely to become more stable instead. These policy actions are discussed in Chapter 4.

The results of the present analysis are conveniently illustrated in Fig. 7, using inequality (2.35) for positive values for

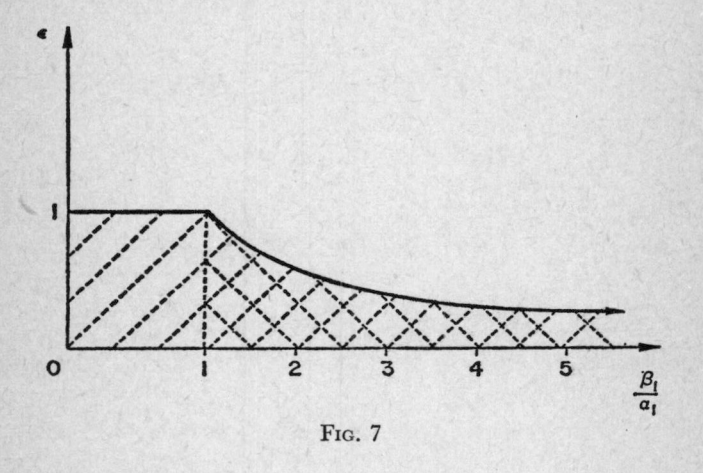

FIG. 7

β_1/a_1 only. The range of values satisfying the $0 < \beta_1/a_1 < 1$ condition is represented by the hatched area. The range of values for $\beta_1/a_1 > 1$, consistent with inequality (2.35), is given by the cross-hatched area, where as $\epsilon \to 0$, $\{(2/\epsilon) - 1\} \to + \infty$. As can be seen now, stability conditions are widened.

CONCLUSION

The naïve Cobweb model assumes all production of a particular good to be offered for sale in the market at discrete

42

points in time. Prices are assumed to respond with infinite velocity to disequilibrium situations to match quantity demanded to available supply. No other price than the short-run market clearing price will ever rule the market, hence no trading takes place at disequilibrium values because all transactors know the market clearing price.

However, few markets, if any, work like this. First of all, prices do not respond with infinite velocity to excess demand situations and over the period that excess demand is measured, trading will occur at different (false) prices especially when the trading period is long. The effect of trading at false prices is a redistribution of purchasing power from buyers to sellers or vice versa. Although the income effects of such changes on the demand curve, which will shift, may be small, it may cause a certain degree of indeterminateness in the market, Hicks [36]. In real markets nobody has sufficient information about all determinants affecting the trade and nobody knows for sure what the best action is. Traders may thus become reluctant to initiate a price change when trading seems disappointing and markets may not be cleared.

Complications of dynamic adjustment, uncertainty, and frictions are easily assumed away in static theory. Newer developments in economic theory on the other hand stress the importance of adjustment, uncertainty and transaction costs. The Cobweb model is just a first step in the development of micro-dynamic theory by concentrating on intertemporal adjustment processes, but it still ignores the aspects of price adjustment under uncertainty, during each trading period.

RECOMMENDED READING

The dynamics of adjustment processes is very well explained by Goodwin [29], in showing the analogy with 'error-control' systems, Arrow and Capron [5], and Henderson and Quandt [34].

Most fascinating but more difficult is the literature on the 'new-microeconomics'. Readers are well advised to study

Stigler [71], Alchian [1] and articles by Hey [35] and Rothschild [64]. Another excellent, but not easy, survey of research on lags in economic behaviour is Nerlove [58].

3 Macro-Disequilibrium Economics

INTRODUCTION

Macro-disequilibrium economics deals traditionally with systems such as the dynamic multiplier, the multiplier–accelerator mechanism and inventory models. More recently a fascinating development in economic analysis has taken place, centred around markets operating under conditions of insufficient information. The implications for macro-economics are most important. A discussion of the 'new' macro-disequilibrium analysis based on the 'Keynes versus Classics' controversy is therefore included.

The conventional 'Keynes versus Classics' debate is usually dealt with in a comparative static way. Expectations are assumed to be unit elastic and unemployment is explained by institutional rigidities in wages, prices or interest rates. The question is whether Keynes is properly interpreted as a comparative static theorist, and whether his attack on Neo-Classical economics was allegedly more than a 'correction' of the Neo-Classical model for certain rigidities. The view expressed by many authors these days is that Keynes's theory is fundamentally different from the Neo-Classical approach. Institutional rigidities were not assumed to explain a situation of underemployment, but, rather, inelastic expectations, based on insufficient information, were, on the current interpretation, Keynes's explanation.

THE DYNAMIC MULTIPLIER

The simplest of all macro-disequilibrium models is undoubtedly the dynamic multiplier, yet in spite of its simplicity it may not be too 'unrealistic'. Recent discussions of adjustment systems in macro-economics show clearly the relevance of dynamic multiplier processes as a form of quantity adjustment in disequilibrium situations.

The assumptions of multiplier theory regard both the supply and demand conditions in an economy. On the supply side the assumptions are: perfectly elastic supply of output, labour and money, and negligible capacity effects of investment spending. Changes in the stock of assets are therefore not taken into account. On the demand side, for simplicity, only two components are distinguished: investment and consumption demand. A discussion of the factors determining investment spending will be postponed for the time being. All investment is exogenous and denoted by I. The demand for consumer goods is linearly related to income.

$$C_t = a_1 Y_t + a_0. \tag{3.1}$$

The demand and supply sides of the economy are not independent. They are linked by a (short-run) equilibrium condition or accounting identity

$$Y_t = C_t + I_t. \tag{3.2}$$

Equations (3.1) and (3.2) together constitute a static model; no lags are involved. The solution is a relation in which one of the endogenous variables C_t, Y_t has been reduced to an explicit expression of the two parameters a_0, a_1 and the exogenous variable I_t. Hence

$$Y_t = (I_t + a_0)/(1 - a_1) \tag{3.3}$$

is a reduced form equation which tells us how the *equilibrium* level of income changes as either autonomous investment or consumption changes.

The dynamic multiplier is not a tool to deal with equilibrium changes, but with disequilibrium processes. Two modifications need to be made to transform the equilibrium model into a disequilibrium one. First, the equilibrium condition (3.2) will have to be reviewed, and second, an error-adjustment process has to be introduced. This can be done in many ways. Here the error-adjustment mechanism will be represented by a one-period delay in the consumption function. This is usually interpreted as a case of extrapolative expectations. Thus

$$C_t = a_1 Y_{t-1} + a_0 \qquad (3.4)$$

will replace equation (3.1).

As we learned earlier, a one-period delay in the consumption function implies that an increase in income in period $t(\Delta Y_t)$ will not add to consumer spending and, since consumer plans are always realised, the amount is therefore saved. But are these intended savings? Assume savings behaviour is also related to the previous level of income

$$S^*{}_t = (1 - a_1) Y_{t-1} - a_0 \qquad (3.5)$$

From this it follows

$$S^*{}_t = Y_{t-1} - C_t$$

but from (3.2) comes

$$S_t = Y_t - C_t$$

Hence, two concepts of savings are involved in a disequilibrium model. One concept, which refers to the difference between Y_t and C_t, represents realised or *ex-post* savings, and the other, which refers to a behavioural assumption like equation (3.5), represents *ex-ante* or planned savings.[1]

The difference between *ex-post* and *ex-ante* savings is

$$(Y_t - C_t) - (Y_{t-1} - C_t) = \Delta Y_t = \text{unintended savings,}$$

which is the amount needed to finance the increase in (realised) investment that brought about the change in income. *Ex-post* savings (intended + unintended savings) always equals investment but *ex-ante* savings will not always do so because of the lag in the savings function. This is why as an equilibrium condition in a dynamic context equation (3.2) is inappropriate. It only refers to short-run equilibrium conditions where *ex-post* savings equal investment, which holds in each period whether income is rising or falling, but it does not imply

[1] The same type of distinction could be made for investment when a production lag is assumed, Allen ([2] pp. 18–19).

income equilibrium. The condition for income equilibrium is equality between S^*_t and I_t. This is easily demonstrated.

Substituting equation (3.4) into (3.2) gives

$$Y_t = aY_{t-1} + a_0 + I_t \tag{3.6}$$

and after subtracting Y_{t-1} from both sides of the equation we obtain

$$\Delta Y_t = I_t - (Y_{t-1} - aY_{t-1} - a_0)$$

which equals

$$\Delta Y_t = I_t - S^*_t. \tag{3.7}$$

The level of income is constant when *ex-ante* savings equal realised investment. Income will increase when realised investment exceeds planned savings, and unintended savings take place. This happens because savers were extrapolating previous (lower) income. On the other hand, when planned savings are greater than realised investment we get a process of income contraction. Savers over-estimate expected income for each period and since in our system investment is always realised, total savings will adjust. This process will continue until *ex-ante* savings reaches a value equal to realised investment. The dynamic multiplier model thus contains a feedback system. The error, i.e. the difference between *ex-ante* and *ex-post* savings (realised investment), is successively reduced to zero through variations in income.

The importance of the dynamic multiplier is that it can show quite clearly which different conclusions will be reached when, for instance, the government intends to spend an extra amount, financed by a budget deficit, for one period only or as a continuing outlay. The static multiplier (equation (3.3)) can, in the first case, only tell us that equilibrium levels of incomes both before and a while after the temporary investment injection will be equal. This implies unchanged income levels in between. The dynamic multiplier can, on the other hand, not only show that after n multiplier rounds where $n = 1, 2, ..., \infty$, the same initial income level will be reached, but it can also show that income in the meantime has been raised even after the investment injection had stopped.

To find out by how much income is raised in each period, we recall equation (3.6)

$$Y_t = a_1 Y_{t-1} + a_0 + I_t$$

and assume that the increase in government expenditure is reflected in a change in I_t. The income increase in period t is:

$$Y_t - Y_0 = \Delta I_t$$

where Y_0 is the initial equilibrium level in period $t-1$.

In the next period, income increases because a fraction, a_1, of the income increase in the previous period will be spent. It is furthermore assumed, for use of the calculations, that investment remains at the higher level, hence

$$Y_{t+1} = Y_0 + \Delta I_t + a_1(Y_t - Y_0) = Y_0 + \Delta I_t + a_1 \Delta I_t$$

Similarly in the next period

$$\begin{aligned} Y_{t+2} &= Y_0 + \Delta I_t + a(Y_{t+1} - Y_0) \\ &= Y_0 + \Delta I_t + a_1 \Delta I_t + a_1{}^2 \Delta I_t \end{aligned}$$

After n periods, where $n = 1, 2, \ldots, \infty$

$$Y_{t+n} = Y_0 + \Delta I_t + a_1 \Delta I_t + a_1{}^2 \Delta I_t + \ldots + a_1{}^{n-1} \Delta I_t + a_1{}^n \Delta I_t$$

and, rearranging

$$Y_{t+n} - Y_0 = \Delta I_t(1 + a_1 + a_1{}^2 + \ldots + a_1{}^{n-1} + a_1{}^n)$$

The right-hand side of the equation represents a geometric series with a common ratio a_1. Applying the summing formula, assuming $0 < a_1 < 1$, will then give the dynamic multiplier

$$Y_{t+n} - Y_0 = \frac{1 - a_1{}^n}{1 - a_1} \Delta I_t, \tag{3.7}$$

which will enable us to find the income increment in each period and not equilibrium values only. The marginal propensity to spend is, on theoretical grounds, non-negative and not greater than one. All adjustment processes with a one-period delay are therefore stable processes. After a disturbance a new equilibrium is always found.

THE MULTIPLIER–ACCELERATOR MODEL

The number of possible adjustment paths, generated by a dynamic multiplier process, is for realistic values of the marginal propensity to spend, given a simple one-period lag, rather small.[1] More interesting cases of dynamic adjustment arise when more complicated lag structures are used. One example is the multiplier–accelerator model, as formulated by Samuelson [65] in which investment is no longer treated as completely autonomous, but related to changes in consumption expenditures.[2] Here, Hicks's [37] reformulation of the model is followed. It is again assumed that the demand for output is of two kinds, consumption C and investment I, hence

$$Y_t = C_t + I_t \qquad (3.8)$$

and that consumption is a linear function of lagged income

$$C_t = a_0 + a_1 Y_{t-1} \qquad (3.9)$$

where $0 < a_1 < 1$ and a_0 is autonomous consumption. Investment is, according to the acceleration principle, related to changes in the level of output. No net investment is needed, only replacement investment to produce a constant level of output. Gross investment is thus positive. An increase in the level of output requires positive net investment. Gross investment, and this is what we actually observe, may therefore increase faster than does output, hence[3]

$$I_t = \beta_1(Y_{t-1} - Y_{t-2}) + \beta_0 \qquad (3.10)$$

where β_1 has a time dimension.[4]

Solution of the model yields a second-order difference equation

[1] See Appendix.

[2] Other examples are found as early as 1936 in the work of Tinbergen [77] and [78].

[3] Reasons for using a lagged accelerator are delivery lags, etc. (see Junankar [43]).

[4] The value of β_1 increases as the relevant period decreases!

50

$$Y_t = (a_1 + \beta_1)Y_{t-1} - \beta_1 Y_{t-2} + (a_0 + \beta_0) \qquad (3.11)$$

and a wide range of possible outcomes, depending largely on the relative values of the propensity to consume and the accelerator coefficient, can be generated. Again we can raise the question of what might happen to the economy once the government has increased investment spending. Output will immediately rise by the same amount as investment, but consumption remains constant until the next period, when it will rise by $a_1 \Delta Y$. Induced investment will rise too, by $\beta_1 \Delta Y$, and output consequently increases even faster. Consumption continues to rise, at an even faster rate, two periods after the increase in output, but investment growth levels off due to the $-\beta_1 Y_{t-2}$ term and will reach a peak value. The rate of increase in output decreases too and a turning point is soon reached. When output starts to decrease $(\Delta Y < 0)$ it will affect investment spending. Two periods later induced investment becomes negative. However, as soon as output starts to decline, endogenous forces start to counteract this movement because of the $-\beta_1 Y_{t-2}$ term now stimulating investment spending. Output will increase slightly and an upward movement will appear; a cyclical pattern could emerge over time. An interesting feature of the model is that investment leads output. Peaks and troughs are reached in investment spending before they appear in output.

Having sketched the possibility of a cyclical pattern in the income generating process, we can now ask which error-adjustment process the multiplier–accelerator model implies. In contrast with the multiplier analysis however, we may envisage the dynamics of the multiplier–accelerator model as a stock adjustment process, rather than a flow adjustment process alone. An autonomous investment injection increases output and changes the desired stock of capital, according to accelerator theory. If the desired stock exceeds the actual stock of capital then positive investment will occur to reduce the difference (error). Positive induced investment raises income even further and therefore raises the desired stock of capital. But additions to the actual stock may proceed at a faster rate than the increase in the desired stock. At some point in time the actual stock could exceed the desired stock. In such a case the error-adjustment mechanism will reduce the rate of induced investment or will even make it negative, until both stocks are equalised. It is this error-reduction process that generates a whole set of different stock adjustment processes through time.

Two factors are of essential importance to the multiplier-accelerator model: first, the appearance of the $-Y_{t-2}$ term to determine turning points and second, the value of α_1 relative to β_1. This is now to be explored.

The solution of the second-order difference equation (3.11) is[1]

$$Y_t = \bar{Y} + A_1(\lambda_1)^t + A_2(\lambda_2)^t \qquad (3.12)$$

where $\bar{Y}$ is the static equilibrium solution, A_1 and A_2 are the arbitrary constants, and

$$\lambda_{1,2} = \frac{(\alpha_1 + \beta_1) \pm \{(\alpha_1 + \beta_1)^2 - 4\beta_1\}^{1/2}}{2}$$

Cycles will occur if

$$\beta_1 > \frac{(\alpha_1 + \beta_1)^2}{4}$$

or if

$$\{1 - (1 - \alpha_1)^{1/2}\}^2 < \beta_1 < \{1 + (1 - \alpha_1)^{1/2}\}^2 \qquad (3.13)$$

This inequality enables us to divide the whole field of values for α_1 and β_1 into two regions, one encompassing values for α_1 and β_1 generating cyclical patterns, and another generating monotonic processes (see Fig. 8). Two more regions can be found by dropping a perpendicular through $\beta_1 = 1$. Values for $\beta_1 < 1$ yield stable processes whether cyclical or not, and values for $\beta_1 > 1$ generate unstable processes. If $\alpha_1 = 0$, then a range of values for β_1 from 0 to 4 will satisfy the cycle condition. The higher the value of the marginal propensity to consume the smaller the range of values for β_1 that satisfies the cycle inequality. Students often think it is the interaction between accelerator *and* multiplier that makes cyclical be-

[1] See Appendix.

52

haviour possible. This is not correct. A lagged accelerator is a necessary condition only, and positive α_1 values just reduce the probability of getting any cycles.

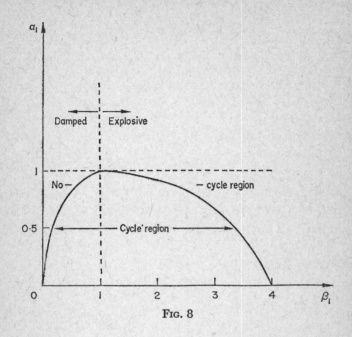

FIG. 8

AN INVENTORY MODEL

A series of models with different lag structures, but all based on the Lundberg demand–output lag, were developed by Metzler [52]. The output lag was quite popular among the pioneers of trade-cycle studies, e.g. Frisch [26], Kalecki [44] and Lundberg [49]. The lag implies production in a period to be different from what is actually sold, when incomes are changing. Where incomes are rising, sales will exceed output and stocks are run down, unintended disinvestment occurs. On the other hand, stocks will rise unintentionally when incomes are falling. Since it is inventory stocks rather than savings which bear the brunt of the disequilibrium process,

Metzler's models are labelled *inventory models*. The model we choose to discuss assumes demand for consumer goods to be linearly related to income ($\equiv$ output in the absence of an output–income lag) and the most recent rate of change, hence

$$C_t = a_1 Y_t + \eta(a_1 Y_t - a_1 Y_{t-1}) \tag{3.14}$$

where a_1 is the marginal propensity to consume and η is the coefficient of expectations. Since output is assumed to depend on sales Z in the previous period we also have

$$Y_t = Z_{t-1} \tag{3.15}$$

Substitution into equation (3.14) gives

$$C_t = a_1 Z_{t-1} + \eta(a_1 Z_{t-1} - a_1 Z_{t-2}) \tag{3.16}$$

and a lagged accelerator mechanism is revealed. All spending, apart from consumption, is autonomous and denoted by I so that

$$Z_t = C_t + I \tag{3.17}$$

represents aggregate demand. Also

$$Y_t - Z_t = V_t \tag{3.18}$$

that is to say, unintended investment in inventories V is related to the difference between output and demand. Inventories are passive; no attempt whatsoever is made by the entrepreneurs to maintain inventory stocks at a desired 'normal' level. To obtain the solution of the model, equation (3.16) is substituted into (3.17). The reduced form in Z is a second-order difference equation

$$Z = (a_1 + \eta a_1)Z_{t-1} - \eta a_1 Z_{t-2} + I \tag{3.19}$$

Again we would like to know which adjustment processes can be expected once an increase in I has raised aggregate demand to a level higher than aggregate output. A process is set in motion leading to a faster rate of growth in output in the next period. Two periods after the shock, the $-\eta a_1 Z_{t-2}$ term will have a depressing effect on the increase in consumer demand, unless η is very small. Output, lagging one period, will rise too, the initial decrease in inventories is stopped, and a turning point reached. The slowing down in the increase in aggregate demand will decrease consumption even further. Inventories start to rise but demand reaches a turning point and will decrease. The $-\eta a_1 \mathcal{Z}_{t-2}$ term will, however, set a lower limit to negative changes in aggregate demand and another turning point will be reached. Fluctuations will continue until, after many periods, the system approaches a final equilibrium. The model is always stable so long as values for a_1 and η are restricted by $0 < a_1,\ \eta < 1$. The field of possible values for a_1 and η is divided into two regions as in Fig. 9, where the dividing line is determined by the equality

$$\eta = \{a_1(1+\eta)^2\}/4$$

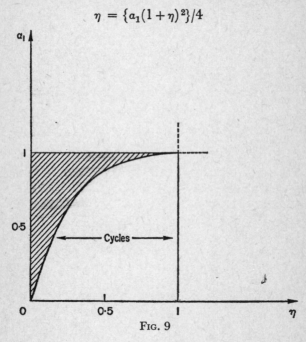

Fig. 9

For the values of η and a_1 lying in the hatched area, monotonic adjustment sequences will result. For other values, oscillations appear. The probability of getting oscillations increases with higher values for η. Where $\eta = 0$ the model collapses to the

55

dynamic multiplier sequence, due to extrapolative expectations.

This stresses once more the importance of the particular lag structure representing an error-adjustment mechanism. The mechanism itself only shows which adjustment paths can be expected, it does not give a justification for the existence of a lag structure. The reasons for lags should be given by economic analysis.

THE NEO-CLASSICAL APPROACH

The standard Neo-Classical model consists of three sectors: a demand sector (equations (3.20)–(3.22)), a monetary sector (3.23), (3.24) and a supply sector including a labour market (3.25)–(3.27).

$$c = c(r), \qquad c'(r) < 0 \tag{3.20}$$
$$i = i(r) \qquad i'(r) < 0 \tag{3.21}$$
$$y = c + i \tag{3.22}$$

$$M^D = kpy \tag{3.23}$$
$$M^D = M^s, \qquad M^s = \text{exogenous} \tag{3.24}$$

$$y = y(N, \bar{K}), \quad \bar{K} = \text{exogenous}, y'(N) > 0, y''(N) < 0 \tag{3.25}$$
$$y'(N) = w, \tag{3.26}$$
$$N = N(w), \qquad N'(w) > 0, \tag{3.27}$$

where c is real consumption, i is real investment, y is real income, r is the rate of interest, w is the real wage rate, M^D is the demand for balances, M^s is the money stock, p is the price level, N is the labour force, and K is the capital stock.

Solving equations (3.26) and (3.27) for the labour market, assuming wage flexibility, will give the real wage rate at full employment level. The level of income (output) is then determined by the given capital stock and the full employment level. Given the level of production, equations (3.20), (3.21) and (3.22) will determine the rate of interest, and the levels of consumption and investment. The equilibrium condition in the money market then determines the price level. The model is fully determinate; there is only one price level at which all sectors are in simultaneous equilibrium at the full employment level of real income, given the money supply and the historically given capital stock. The equilibrium position is graphically represented in Fig. 10 (solid lines).

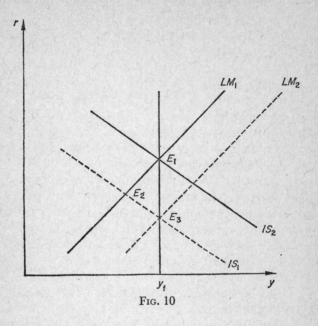

Fig. 10

Suppose now that entrepreneurial expectations take a turn for the worse, so that at any rate of interest investment demand is lower. The *IS* schedule will consequently shift to the left (dotted line). The *IS* curve now intersects the *LM* curve at point E_2 left of the full-employment level of output. There is thus a situation of excess supply in the goods market, leading to a downward pressure on the price level and an excess supply for money that will bring interest rates down. The falling price level is a shift parameter in the money market and will push the *LM* curve to the right until it intersects the *IS* curve at the full-employment level of real income at E_3. The rate of interest and the price level are lower than before in the new equilibrium. Real income is unchanged but investment and thus savings are both lower while the output of

57

consumer goods has increased.[1] Real wages and employment are not affected.

Now why is it that Neo-Classical economists have such full confidence that an equilibrium situation will be reached after the occurrence of a parametric disturbance? The essential trick of their trade is a system of perfectly flexible wages and prices brought about by a *tâtonnement* process. Leijonhufvud pointed out: 'The "automatic" functioning of the system in Classical theory depends on the efficient performance of both roles – *prices should disseminate the information* necessary to co-ordinate the economic activities and plans of independent transaction units, and *prices should provide the incentives* for transaction units to adjust their activities in such a manner that they become consistent in the aggregate' ([47] p. 393).

Now it is not the effectiveness of price incentives that we are to discuss here, but the informational role of prices. What entrepreneurs, workers and bondholders, in short, transactors, want to know is whether the set of market prices they face are the 'best' they can obtain and whether at these prices every quantity they planned to trade can be sold or bought. In other words a transactor wants to know whether market prices are full equilibrium prices. But who knows the equilibrium price once the economy has been disturbed? The Neo-Classical theorists solved the problem with the introduction of a special *tâtonnement* process. What it implies is this: once a disturbance from the equilibrium values happens an auctioneer (who can be thought of as a personification of the 'invisible hand') announces a new set of prices, so-called *prix criés au hasard*, to get a feel of the market. He will then register for each good whether demand and supply match. If not, he will announce a new set with higher prices for markets exhibiting excess demand and lower prices for those with excess supply. Again bids and offers are received and compared, and again an attempt will be made to clear all markets

[1] Note that if consumption was made dependent on income, both consumption and investment would have been the same as before. The fall in interest rates would have been sufficient to offset the effects of a lowered expected rate of return on investment.

simultaneously by announcing an adjusted set of prices. None of the offers are binding unless the announced set of prices turns out to be the equilibrium set. If it does not then all transactors may withdraw and await a new call by the auctioneer. The *tâtonnement* process has a recontracting arrangement. This arrangement serves a special purpose: it guarantees that the *tâtonnement* process will continue until a final equilibrium is arrived at and it prevents the final equilibrium from being affected by non-equilibrium, intermediate transactions made *en route*. The auctioneer could thus be visualised as a fast-working computer, reducing the error in all markets in an iterative adjustment process (see Goodwin [29]). Prices adjust with infinite velocity to disequilibrium situations.

THE ECONOMICS OF KEYNES

What happens if there is no auctioneer? Transactors no longer have full information so that non-equilibrium transactions will be made. Recontracting, when transactors discover a mistake, is impossible. Each transactor has to decide for himself whether to accept an offer or not with a risk of striking a bad bargain. He is no longer a price taker, but can set his own price in an attempt to maximise his income. If this is the situation most relevant to the world in which we are living, what will happen once the economy is thrown off its original equilibrium position? Since prices do not adjust fast enough what other mechanism will bring back a new full-employment equilibrium?

In order to compare the Keynesian analysis with the outcome of the Neo-Classical framework, the same type of initial disturbance is assumed: entrepreneurial expectations take a turn for the worse. A lower expected rate of return on investment projects will lead to a reduction in planned investment expenditures, and a situation of excess supply is created in the capital-goods market. Capital-goods producing entrepreneurs face an unexpected decline in sales. In the bond market a situation of excess demand will arise since savers had not yet anticipated the reduction in the issue of new bonds (to finance investment). Excess supply will prevail in the money markets also. The crucial question is now how far and how fast interest rates and goods prices will come down and bond prices go up to restore equilibrium. Let us take each market in turn.

The entrepreneur who faces a decline in his sales does not know for sure whether the decline is a temporary or permanent one, so he waits to absorb more information. When things turn out to be of a more permanent character he will obtain his information in the form of unsold goods – i.e. unintended inventories begin to pile up. He may then decide to reduce the scale of production or to cut down the selling price of his products. But will he take the latter step? In a case of uncertainty, where the entrepreneur is not told in the beginning of each marketing period what the market clearing price will be, he has to form his own opinion. He undoubtedly remembers the prices he dealt at in the past, and some form of an average normal price concept may have developed in his mind. Consequently, when prices start to fall, they diverge from this normal level. The entrepreneur considers it more likely for the normal price to prevail in the end and therefore expects future prices to be higher again than the current lower prices. He is said to have *inelastic price expectations*. He will not lower his selling price immediately to match his supply to demand. Instead, he will adjust his output, reduce inputs and unemployed resources are created. Now what happens to the bondholder? He is faced with a situation of excess demand for bonds, resulting in a downward pressure on interest rates. But bondholders have inelastic expectations too, being risk averters, and expect bond prices to come down again. A capital gain is made by selling now and hoarding the proceeds. But prospective buyers also have inelastic expectations and the prospects of a capital loss may not be too encouraging to force them into the market. They stay liquid. There may be some fall in the rate of interest but it is not likely to be sufficient to equate savings to investment. The restricted fall in the rate of interest is the result of a greater preference for liquidity. The consequence is a further drop in the demand for investment goods, since neither capital-goods prices nor interest rates have come down sufficiently. More unemployed resources emerge.

Let us now take the unemployed worker. Having been laid off he wants to know whether this is a temporary or a permanent phenomenon. He may be able to find a job immediately at a wage rate much lower than he experienced before but will not take it. He too has developed a normal expected wage rate, his reservation price, and will only accept an adjustment of his reservation price with a lengthening of his unemployment. He will first start a search for jobs balancing the costs of search, his forgone earnings, against the benefits of extended search. When he finally realises that the unemployment situation is a more serious one, he will lower his reservation price somewhat and accept a job at this rate when further search seems useless. In the meantime he has not contributed to the production of goods. His consumption expenditures have decreased and more workers are laid off as a result.

All the transactors seem to have decided not to cut back on prices but instead to rely on a policy of quantity adjustment in response to disequilibrium situations. The outcome of such a process is well known: a contracting dynamic multiplier process is set in motion, leading to an ultimate position far worse than the initial disturbance would suggest. The multiplier, as a deviation-amplifying process, is the outcome of a form of behaviour based on inelastic expectations, leading to higher levels of unemployment.[1] Clower [14], and Leijonhufvud [47], argue most convincingly that the dynamic adjustment approach, as just discussed, represents better what Keynes could have had in mind when writing his General Theory, than does the comparative static approach. Keynesian analysis is pure disequilibrium analysis, applicable to a world of insufficient information.

---

[1] Stigler [71], [72], and Alchian [1] showed utility or wealth maximising behaviour in open unconstrained markets to be perfectly consistent with a 'slow' reacting price.

RECOMMENDED READING

A useful discussion and survey of trade-cycle theory and evidence is given by Rau [62]; highly recommended, but more technical, is Evans [20].

Leijonhufvud [47] is of course the standard text for a discussion of Keynes's ideas. A shorter version is available [48], as is a study by Hines [39].

An important contribution to the comparison of Neo-Classical and Keynesian models in Hicks's [38] discussion of Fixprice and Flexprice methods.

4 Stabilisation Policy

INTRODUCTION

In a Neo-Classical world governed by the omniscient auctioneer the need for policy seems absent and transactors just hop blithely from one set of equilibrium values to another. Any error due to an unanticipated exogenous disturbance is eliminated with almost embarrassing speed. No values are observed other than equilibrium values. The world seems perfect.

Walrasian or Neo-Classical general equilibrium analysis is an exercise in *ideal state* economics. It shows the interdependence of all markets and the role of prices in solving problems of distribution, allocation and production. In this way it has added tremendously to our knowledge of the operation of a market economy under highly idealised conditions.

These highly idealised conditions do not apply to the real world; as a consequence we are continuously reminded that 'frictions' occur. In all acquired statistics on the economy not a single equilibrium set has been found. What has been measured all the time are these frictions or deviations from equilibrium values, such as accelerating house prices, changing levels of employment and either deficits or surpluses on the balance of payments. These frictions are generally not appreciated and economic policy is called for. But to base policy on a static equilibrium model of the economy seems absurd. It presupposes a situation that is non-existent and it assumes a feedback sufficiently strong to guide the economy to a new equilibrium level relatively quickly.

When a certain amount of unemployment is measured in a particular period we do not have a good starting point for economic policy unless we know what the most likely future development of unemployment will be when no action is taken. The observed amount of unemployment is not the final result of a multiplier process that has come to an end, but the outcome of a whole range of interacting forces starting many periods back and most likely to continue for many periods ahead. Only when the policy-makers know which particular disequilibrium model explains the observed patterns best could they, with carefully balanced variations in fiscal policy in the appropriate periods, increase stabilisation.

There are in fact two ways in which a government could act: they can, by direct intervention, control market prices and the circular flow of income, or they could try to adjust the expectations of those who by their actions affect the outcome of economic processes. This policy is often used to encourage entrepreneurs to invest and to discourage speculation by dealers in currency markets, for instance by repeatedly denying that a possible devaluation is at hand.

In this chapter we shall first give an example of how the government could intervene in a market by influencing traders' expectations. We shall then discuss some interesting results of direct government intervention in a macro-dynamic framework.

MICRO-STABILISATION POLICY

Substantial price fluctuations can occur in markets when demand is highly inelastic and supply is affected by random disturbances such as weather and pests. Price changes may cause undesired changes in the distribution of incomes. Higher prices for agricultural products raise farmers' revenues and thus their incomes, but the non-agricultural population suffers from a decline in real income. The redistribution is the other way around of course when farmers have a bumper harvest and prices fall. Not surprisingly in these circumstances governments have intervened to do something about these redistributions. Agricultural stabilisation programmes such as minimum price guarantees, food subsidies and buffer stocks have been designed. They have operated with varying degrees of success.

64

It has also been argued, e.g. by Jesness [41], that farmers' expectations themselves could be a major cause of price fluctuations in certain agricultural markets. In such cases government forecasting of future equilibrium prices could have a stabilising effect. How government forecasting could work out in a Cobweb framework was recently investigated by Devletoglou [17]. Recalling the naïve Cobweb model with extrapolative expectations:

$$q^D{}_t = a_0 - a_1 p_t \qquad (4.1)$$
$$q^s{}_t = \beta_0 + \beta_1 p_{t-1} \qquad (4.2)$$
$$q^D{}_t = q^s{}_t \qquad (4.3)$$

with parametric conditions $a_1,\ \beta_1 > 0$, and with a solution

$$p_t = (p_0 - \bar{p})\left(-\frac{\beta_1}{a_1}\right)^t + \bar{p} \qquad (4.4)$$

where $\bar{p} \neq p_0$.

Now it could be assumed that quantity supplied in period t is not only a function of actual lagged market price but also of the predicted market clearing price $p^f{}_t$. The supply equation would then be:

$$q^s{}_t = \beta_1\{\mu p^f{}_t + (1-\mu)p_{t-1}\} + \beta_0 \qquad (4.5)$$

where $0 \leqslant \mu \leqslant 1$.

In the case where $\mu = 0$, suppliers have no confidence at all in the price forecasted by the government, and the model is reduced to the standard naïve Cobweb model. Suppliers prefer to rely on their own knowledge of history which extends to one period only. Suppliers on the other hand show blind confidence in the government's predictive ability and disregard their own experience completely in the case where $\mu = 1$. Hence $p^e{}_t = p^f{}_t$. Solving the model for p_t in terms of the initial condition, the parameters and the equilibrium price $\bar{p}$, assuming the forecast to be correct,[1] hence $p_t = p^f{}_t$, gives

$$p_t = (p_0 - \bar{p})\left\{-\frac{\beta_1(1-\mu)}{a_1 - \beta_1\mu}\right\}^t + \bar{p} \qquad (4.6)$$

with a stability condition

[1] The formal possibility of a correct public forecast was analysed by Grunberg and Modigliani [31].

$$\left| -\frac{\beta_1(1-\mu)}{a_1 - \beta_1\mu} \right| < 1 \qquad (4.7)$$

The same stability condition as in the naïve Cobweb model is, not surprisingly, obtained when $\mu = 0$. In the case where suppliers accept unconditionally the correct market price announced by the government, we see that μ will equal unity and the model reaches equilibrium instantaneously. The relative slopes of demand and supply curves do not matter any more. All transactors know the market clearing price; there is no search or uncertainty. We have in fact returned to the realm of the Neo-Classical auctioneer where disequilibrium processes are banned. The intermediate cases where $0 < \mu < 1$, are therefore of more interest for disequilibrium analysis.

Comparing equation (4.4) with (4.6) shows an improvement in the stability of the latter system, where nominator and denominator are reduced by the same amounts $-\beta_1\mu$. This does not imply that positive values for μ always transform an unstable process into a stable one. The minimum value for μ to change an unstable process into a stable one is calculated from equation (4.7) as

$$\mu < \frac{+(\beta_1/a_1)}{2(\beta_1/a_1)} \qquad (4.8)$$

Smaller values do not make unstable systems stable, they only reduce fluctuations to some extent. The field with possible combinations for β_1/a_1 and μ, when $\beta_1/a_1 \geqslant 1$ and $0 \leqslant \mu \leqslant 1$, is displayed in Fig. 11.

The model is always stable when $|\beta_1/a_1| < 1$, whatever value for μ applies. Higher values for μ means that more weight is given to correct public forecasts at the expense of the influence of past prices. An already stable Cobweb will converge even faster. Fluctuations are reduced though still divergent, for values of $\beta_1/a_1 > 1$ and $\mu < 1$ to the left of the border line. For values at the right-hand side stable processes are obtained. Correct public forecasting can, assuming the suppliers accept them, reduce instability in markets with a production lag. But what happens if the odd public forecast turns out to be wrong? Will the value of the coefficient of acceptance drop

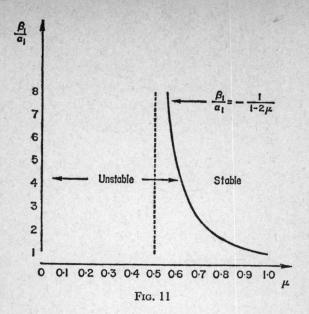

FIG. 11

back to zero immediately? Clearly more analysis is needed to find out how sensitive μ is with respect to errors in public forecasting. For the time being we satisfy ourselves that positive values can, at least, reduce instability and its undesired consequences.

MACRO-STABILISATION POLICY

The idea of a self-adjusting economy based on Say's Law and the quantity theory of money was crudely destroyed by the Keynesian revolution in the middle 1930s. Until then, questions of expansion and contraction were mainly discussed under the heading of trade cycle theory and given the proper monetary environment, periods of expansion were always thought to follow periods of contraction. The conclusion reached in Chapter 3 is a different one. A change in long-run entrepreneurial expectations will push the economy into a deep depression through a multiplier process without a turning point in sight. Government intervention seems unavoidable.

67

Fiscal policy, by means of which changes in income and expenditure flows could be affected directly, became a major tool for stabilisation policy after the Second World War, and monetary policy lost some of its support. The question of whether money does or does not matter is, however, not pursued here. Both kinds of policy are evaluated on their relative merit in dealing with disequilibrium situations.

A question that aroused at least as much controversy was whether stabilisation policy should be carried out by rules or by discretionary measures. Much of the controversy relies on the presence and character of lags in the economy and thus on the proper timing of policy. This aspect of policy is most important. Let us give an example and consider a hypothetical economy in which investment has been temporarily cut back due to pessimistic expectations. The time path of national income could show up as in Fig. 12, for Y'. Before national income will eventually have caught up again with its previous equilibrium level income is forgone in the transition period. Thus, as soon as income starts to decline, and unemployment to rise, the government is called in and asked to do something.[1] To measure the effects of any action that is taken a 'policy-on' variable Z_t is introduced in a simple multiplier model such that

$$Z_t = Y_t + G_t \qquad (4.9)$$

where G_t represents *compensating* government expenditure. The other two equations of the model are:

$$C_t = aZ_{t-1} \qquad (4.10)$$

and

$$Y_t = C_t + I_t \qquad (4.11)$$

In the initial equilibrium $Z_t = Y_t = 2000$, $I_t = 400$ and $a = 0.8$. In period $t+1$, investment drops to 200 and stays at this lower level for two more periods, then investors' confidence is sufficiently restored to increase investment expendi-

---

[1] Note that in this model we are only concerned with fiscal policy.

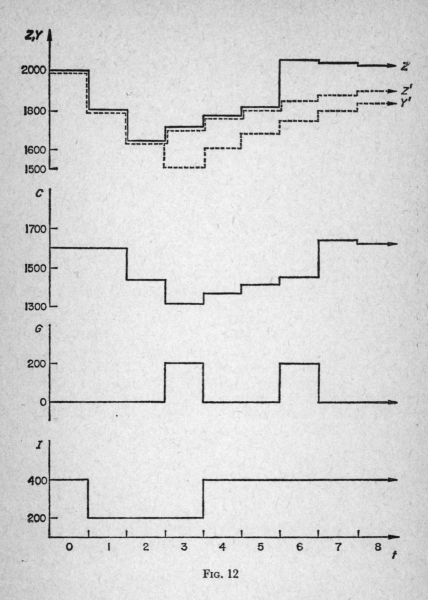

Fig. 12

tures back to the initial 400 level. The effects on the economy
are summarised in Table I.

TABLE I

Period	C	I	Y	G	Z
0	1600	400	2000	0	2000
1	1600	200	1800	0	1800
2	1440	200	1640	0	1640
3	1312	200	1512	200	1712
4	1369·6	400	1769·6	0	1769·6
5	1415·68	400	1815·68	0	1815·68
6	1452·54	400	1852·54	200	2052·54
7	1642·03	400	2042·03	0	2042·03
8	1633·63	400	2033·63	0	2033·63
·	·	·	·	·	·
·	·	·	·	·	·
·	·	·	·	·	·
11	1600	400	2000	0	2000

As the government becomes aware of the fall in income,
some income is already lost forever before compensating
expenditures are materialised in period $t+3$. Income starts
to rise immediately, see time path for Z', but it still seems a
long way before the initial full employment level is reached.
So in a desperate attempt the government again injects purchasing power into the economy now in period 6, but in their
zeal over-estimate the actual amount needed to restore full
employment. National spending overshoots the desired income
mark and inflation could occur. Fortunately the spending
injection had a once and for all character only. A contracting
multiplier process is set in motion as soon as the government
stops spending, and the desired equilibrium level is eventually
reached. This movement is described by the Z path.

The success of government action clearly depends on three
factors:

(1) its timing,
(2) its direction, and
(3) its magnitude.

If either one of the three conditions is not met government action will not be perfectly stabilising or even worse, may be destabilising. Only in the unlikely case where the government foresees exactly timing, direction and magnitude of movements in the 'policy-off' variable Y_t, or some of its components, will it be possible to realise perfect stabilisation. Perfect stabilisation in our example implies $Z_t = Z_{t-1}$, which can be achieved when compensating expenditures are made dependent on income in such a way that any movement in Y is completely neutralised by counter-cyclical expenditures in the same time. Algebraically

$$G_t = -\gamma Y_t, \quad \text{where } \gamma = 1.$$

A more interesting framework to analyse the effects of government policy is the multiplier–accelerator model, since its performance is not restricted to monotonic movements alone. Its solution, in terms of the 'policy-on' variable Z_t is,

$$Z_t - (\alpha_1 + \beta_1)Z_{t-1} + \beta_1 Z_{t-2} = A \qquad (4.12)$$

where A is autonomous consumption α_0, plus autonomous investment β_0, plus compensating government expenditures G_t. Let us moreover assume that equation (4.12) generates a cyclical time path with constant amplitude $\beta_1 = 1$ as in Fig. 13 for 'policy-off' variable Y_t.

A perfect counter-cyclical policy requires a time shape of government expenditures which is exactly the mirror image of the cycle in Y_t. This is algebraically achieved when the equation $G_t = -\gamma Y_t$ is added to the model. Compensating government spending is determined by an endogenous movement in the cycle generating system. In each period a carefully balanced increase or decrease in counter-cyclical spending is added to total spending in the appropriate period, to rule out all undesired deviations from equilibrium income.[1]

Thus from a theoretical point of view, no insurmountable obstacles prevent the achievement of full stabilisation. But the

[1] A corollary of such an example of perfect policy is that correlation between Z_t and G_t is zero, while between Y_t and G_t it is minus unity, assuming a zero trend.

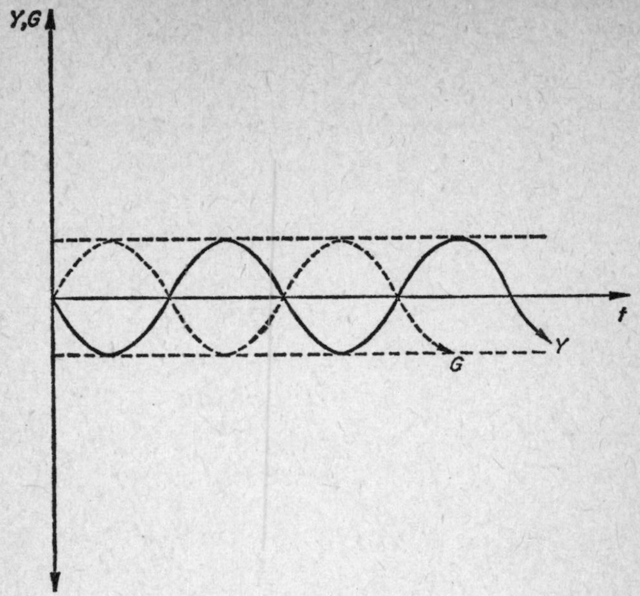

Fig. 13

analysis does already point out the vulnerability of stabilisation policy when actually applied. Compensating expenditures will, when timing is out, either come too late or too early. The effects are not just that no complete stabilisation is achieved, but, and this is worse, the effects can be such that instability is increased. Suppose G_t is 90° out of phase because of lags in the system. Positive counter-cyclical spending does not start until the economy has passed through the trough and reaches its maximum impact when the economy is half-way between peak and trough (compared with the path of policy-off variable Y). Fluctuations in Z will as a consequence show a greater amplitude than fluctuations in Y. This could mean higher inflation in booming periods and more unemployment in a depression.[1]

The example also shows how important it is for policy-makers to know the nature of the disequilibrium process.

[1] Policy-makers will have completely mis-specified the direction of stabilisation policy when G_t is 180° out of phase.

72

With the wrong process in mind attempts to stabilise the economy can hardly have more than a random chance of success. It is possible to carry out a more formal investigation into government action to attain greater stability. We therefore first recall Fig. 19 (p.89) from the Appendix. The vertical axis of the diagram in Fig. 14, labelled a_1, corresponds with $-(\alpha_1 + \beta_1)$

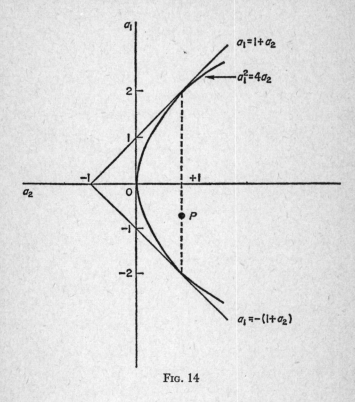

Fig. 14

in equation (4.12), while the horizontal axis labelled a_2, corresponds with β_1. Given the unity value for β_1, we will find all relevant combinations of a_1 and a_2 on the perpendicular through $a_2 = 1$. Given the negative coefficient for Z_{t-1}, we also know that the particular combination that applies to our case will be found in the lower half of the area bounded by

73

the parabola; say point P. Next, policy rule $G_t = -\gamma Y_t$ is substituted into equation (4.12) and we obtain

$$Z_t - (a_1 + \beta_1)(1 - \gamma) Z_{t-1} + \beta_1 (1 - \gamma) Z_{t-2} = (a_0 - \beta_0)(1 - \gamma)$$
(4.13)

which again can be interpreted with the help of Fig. 14.

We know that the strength of government policy is reflected by γ. In those cases where $0 < \gamma \leqslant 1$ we see that stabilisation policy increases the a_1 coefficient with a value $\gamma(a_1 + \beta_1)$, which will make it less negative, while the a_2 coefficient is decreased by $-\gamma \beta_1$. This implies a shift from P into the north-west direction. The higher γ the stronger the shift and the more stable the system. In the extreme case where $\gamma = 1$, the shift is straight towards the point of origin. The system is perfectly stable. Again, perfect timing of policy has been assumed. This is somewhat unsatisfactory, but when lags in government action are taken into account difference equations appear of an order greater than two, which are rather awkward to handle. But with access to fast computation machinery, readers can carry out interesting experiments for hypothetical cases.

An ingenious method to analyse problems of stabilisation policy when government policy is not well timed, was presented by Friedman [21]. In his analysis he used a well-known statistical theorem,[1] through which equation (4.9) which defines 'policy-on' variable Z_t can be transformed to

$$\sigma^2 Z = \sigma^2 Y + \sigma^2 G + 2r_{YG} \sigma_Y \sigma_G$$
(4.14)

in which σ^2, the variance, measures the magnitude of fluctuations and r, the correlation coefficient, measures the 'fit' or timing of policy. When applied to the regular cyclical patterns presented in Fig. 13, we note that G_t and Y_t move in opposite directions and have their turning points in the same periods. Correlation between G_t and Y_t is perfect, $r = -1$. We also note that direction and magnitude of government spending

---

[1] The variance of the sum of two random variables equals the sum of their separate variances only if they are independent (implying zero correlation).

matches exactly any fluctuations in Y_t in such a way as to iron out all fluctuations in Z_t; thus $\sigma^2{}_Y = \sigma^2{}_G$.

On substituting these observations into equation (4.14) we obtain

$$\sigma^2{}_Z = \sigma^2{}_G + \sigma^2{}_G + 2(-1)\sigma^2{}_G = 0$$

which confirms our knowledge that stabilisation policy is perfect in a case like this. Thus two measures, r and σ^2, are available to evaluate the effectiveness of policy and, what is most important, both are not independent. Let us first consider the case when timing is perfect but policy action is not strong enough, though it is aimed in the right direction. Translated into symbols: $r = -1$ and $\sigma^2{}_G < \sigma^2{}_Y$, because the amplitude in counter-cyclical spending is less than the amplitude in national income variations. Obviously $\sigma^2{}_Z$ will no longer equal zero, some variation remains, though to a smaller degree than before.

Important conclusions are reached in another case when both magnitude and direction of policy are considered to be carried out faultlessly, but when timing is wrong. This implies $\sigma^2{}_G = \sigma^2{}_Y$, but $|r| < 1$. Substituting these data into equation (4.14) shows

$$\sigma^2{}_Z = 2\sigma^2{}_G + 2r_{YG}\sigma^2{}_G$$

which does not equal zero since $r > -1$. Although the government accurately predicted the size of the disturbance, stability is not achieved. The more the coefficient of correlation deviates from minus unity the more destabilising policy will be, as reflected in a higher value for $\sigma^2{}_Z$. When timing is faulty, and it is bound to be as we shall see later, it might be better for the government not to attempt to compensate fluctuations fully.

For a given value of r, implying the time lags to be known, an optimum value for $\sigma^2{}_G$ can be found which is less than $\sigma^2{}_Y$. For any other magnitude of compensating expenditures instability is increased. Thus the poorer the timing, the smaller must be the amount of counter-cyclical spending to reduce the likelihood of adverse effects. But Friedman's proposals point in a different direction. Since bad timing is unavoidable

75

and since the government has no perfect knowledge of the extent of future fluctuations, it should avoid discretionary policy altogether and rely completely on rules. Before this argument is carried further, however, we shall first discuss what lags can be held responsible for improper timing.

Consider a time scale as in Fig. 15 and suppose the economy to be in equilibrium in period t. Suppose furthermore that

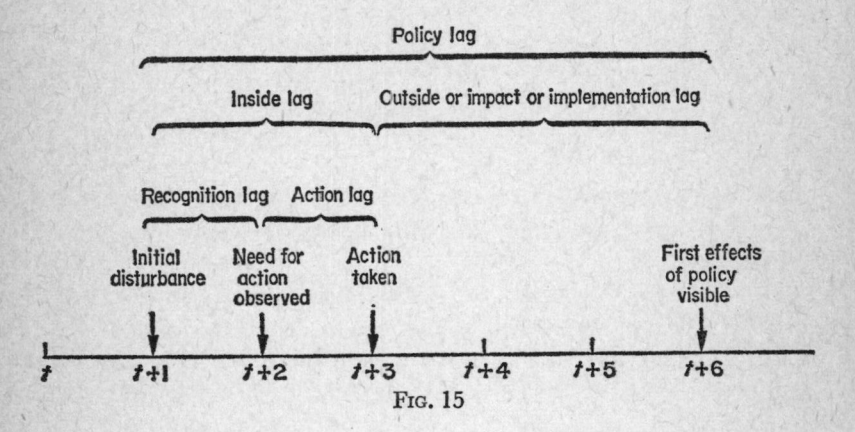

Fig. 15

entrepreneurs cut down on investment expenditure in period $t+1$, due to pessimistic expectations. The undesirable outcome of this behaviour has already been shown. We now have to consider what can be done about it. To meet the decrease in demand so as not to make entrepreneurial expectations self-fulfilling, the government should act immediately. But at this very moment the government has no idea of what processes are going on. Statistical series are published at fixed intervals: some are on a monthly basis, such as employment, exports and industrial production series, some on a quarterly basis, such as G.D.P., stock building and money stock.[1] But an unexpected quarterly increase in manufacturing stocks in a particular quarter does not necessarily imply a worsening

[1] See each issue of *Economic Trends*, a publication of the Central Statistical Office.

of the situation. Economic time series consist of a systematic, a seasonal and a random component, and each one of these components can change independently. The increase in manufacturing stocks can be purely random, in which case precipitating government action can create adverse effects. A correct interpretation of the numbers is often only possible when moving averages are calculated. Thus more up-to-date information is needed to bring the older information into perspective and to detect a possible systematic change,[1] eliminating seasonal and random components. This results in a technical delay before the need for intervention is even recognised. The government could then decide which discretionary action to take. To propose a supplementary budget, a new finance bill, etc. requires further study, parliamentary approval and discussion. The action lag created by these delays is due to the institutional framework in a modern economy. When action is finally taken, it may take up to several periods, months, quarters or even years before the first signs of recovery show up, due to more behavioural, institutional and technological lags. This is the outside lag.

Together, the inside and outside lag can take up quite a long time. This creates two specific disadvantages. Disequilibrium situations will last longer, which is not desirable, but it is also possible when policy measures actually start to produce results, that a different policy is required since other circumstances may have affected the economy in the meantime. Not surprisingly, ways have been looked for to resolve these disadvantages by reducing the policy lag. One way is to shorten the recognition lag with the help of leading indicators. Another is to reduce the action lag by initiating, for instance, taxation changes in advance. But it is also possible to study the 'lagging' characteristics of specific instruments for economic policy and to select those producing quick and fairly certain results.

It is generally argued that the inside lag for monetary policy is relatively short. The monetary authorities are usually able to intervene in the money market at relatively short intervals.

[1] See 'Measuring Variability in Economic Time Series', in *Economic Trends* (Aug. 1972).

The outside lags are much more of a problem. Friedman [23], [25], found lags in monetary policy to be not only long but also variable, ranging from two years to one month, varying for different definitions for the stock of money and for expansionary and contracting periods. Walters [80] found a mean lag of six months for the U.K., for M_1, the narrow definition of money which consists of currency plus bank demand deposits, using pre-1914 data. Crockett's [15] estimates for more recent periods showed lags of twice that size between changes in monetary aggregates and investment expenditures, but for consumption shorter lags were observed.

Inside lags for fiscal policy are generally assumed to be longer when compared with monetary policy. The outside lag is shorter, at least in the U.S., but anyhow less variable.[1] Studies by Hopkin and Godley [40], and Shephard and Surrey [67], showed the effects of tax changes to be almost negligible up to the first two quarters after their implementation. The impact in the second year was double the impact in the first year. In a more recent study by Surrey [74], using the N.I.E.S.R. model, it was found that peak values for G.D.P. occurred in the third and fourth quarter after a direct stimulus of £100 million. G.D.P. would then drop almost asymptotically to a new equilibrium level which is virtually approached after twelve periods.

The undeniable existence of inside lags and the implied danger of improper timing was a strong weapon in the hands of advocates of a policy based on rules, since such a policy would at least reduce the action lag. Friedman formulated several monetary rules, the latest in 1969 [24]. Fiscal rules for stabilisation policy were formulated too. An orthodox rule, from the 1930s, emphasised to maintain a balanced budget irrespective of the state of the economy as a whole. A more modern interpretation is to balance the budget at full-employment revenues. Such a policy relies on automatic stabilisers such as progressive taxation and unemployment insurance. A decline in the level of economic activity automatically triggers

[1] See for instance the study by Rasche and Shapiro [61].

off the payment of unemployment benefits and reduces tax payments, thereby creating a deficit in the government budget. A counter-cyclical increase in expenditure results and fluctuations are lessened. The stabilisers are said to be built into the system since no *ad hoc* government decision is needed to make them optional. This will shorten the action lag. Another form of a built-in stabilising mechanism is formula flexibility. Automatic changes in taxes and public expenditure are then initiated by changes in tax parameters, for instance, legislated in advance. The counter-cyclical movement in taxes and expenditures is, as a result, even stronger than in the constant parameter case.[1] The use of automatic stabilisers is not without pitfalls. First an index or normal level of economic activity to which stabilisers are linked should be chosen. This begs the question of an acceptable rate of unemployment for instance, a rate upon which not everybody agrees. A second problem is that a systematic downward movement actually has to take place before stabilisers start to act and unless strongly leading indicators are used some cyclical movement seems hardly avoidable.

The argument in favour of a policy based on rules because of the shorter inside lag is not very convincing. Discretionary policy, which means action taken at specific points in time which the government sees as appropriate, such as an autumn budget, can also be based on leading indicators or econometric models to forecast turning points. A far stronger argument in favour of a policy based on rules is the variability of lags. The unpredictability of the length of the impact lag makes the timing of policy most hazardous. Yet a policy of rules alone is not without danger either. Under certain rules instability may be increased, as was shown by Phillips [59], [60] and Baumol [6].

Important as automatic stabilisers are in a modern economy, they have been of insufficient strength to prevent four mild recessions in the post-war period. The need for supplementary discretionary measures if carefully used seems obvious. Since

[1] For more detailed discussion see Musgrave [55].

Dow [18] published his study on the *Management of the British Economy*, a long discussion has been going on as to whether fiscal and monetary policy have failed to be stabilising [13], [11]. From the discussions it seems as if stabilisation was the major objective of economic policy. But was it?

RECOMMENDED READING

This chapter, more than the preceding ones, is very sketchy indeed, and the reader is strongly advised to read some of the articles and books to which reference was made. A most useful book on the use of leading indicators and econometric models to help stabilisation policy is Evans [20].

Appendix

LINEAR DIFFERENCE EQUATIONS

The first differences of a series of squared positive integers (1, 4, 9, 16, ...) are 3, 5, 7, 9, ... The second differences are constant and equal to 2. The series of squared positive integers will be denoted by X_1, X_2, X_3, ... There are two ways to express X_t:

(1) as $X_t = t^2$, where t is a positive integer, and

(2) by relating X_t to X_{t-1} and X_{t-2}, as the second differences are constant.

Hence

$$(X_t - X_{t-1}) - (X_{t-1} - X_{t-2}) = 2$$

and

$$X_t - 2X_{t-1} + X_{t-2} = 2 \qquad (A.1)$$

for $t > 2$, and $X_1 = 1$ and $X_2 = 4$ as initial conditions. Equation (A.1) is called a difference equation, it shows a relationship between discrete consecutive values of X.

Generally, an equation of the form

$$X_t + a_1 X_{t-1} + a_2 X_{t-2} + ... + a_n X_{t-n} = f(t) \qquad (A.2)$$

in which a_1, a_2, ..., a_n are constants, $f(t)$ is an arbitrary function of (t) or a constant, and no X term is raised to a power higher or lower than one, is called a linear difference equation with constant coefficients. The order of a difference equation is determined by the difference between the lowest and highest subscripts of X. Equation (A.2) has the order $t - (t-n) = n$.

Solving equation (A.2) means expressing X_t as an exponential function of t alone. It has to meet two requirements:

(1) it should satisfy all initial conditions (= initial values of X); and

(2) it should satisfy the difference equation.

The (general) solution of a difference equation consists of two parts, a homogeneous solution and a particular solution.

The homogeneous solution is the solution of the homogeneous form of equation (A.2) that is a form where $f(t) = 0$. Hence

$$X_t + a_1 X_{t-1} + a_2 X_{t-2} + \ldots + a_n X_{t-n} = 0 \qquad \text{(A.3)}$$

is a homogeneous equation.

The procedure for obtaining the homogeneous solution is as follows. Let $X_t = \lambda^t$, substitute in equation (A.3)

$$\lambda^t + \lambda^{t-1} + \lambda^{t-2} + \ldots + \lambda^{t-n} = 0$$

divide through by λ^{t-n}, and obtain

$$\lambda^n + a_1 \lambda^{n-1} + \ldots + a_n = 0 \qquad \text{(A.4)}$$

The result is called an auxiliary or reduced equation.

The roots of equation (A.4), λ_t, will determine the solution of (A.3) which is written as

$$X = A_1 \lambda^t + A_2 \lambda^t_2 + \ldots + A_n \lambda^t_n \qquad \text{(A.5)}$$

where A_t are constants to be determined in such a way that the initial values of X are satisfied. The procedure for obtaining the particular solution is explained later.

FIRST-ORDER HOMOGENEOUS DIFFERENCE EQUATIONS

Let

$$X_t - a X_{t-1} = 0 \qquad \text{(A.6)}$$

be a first-order homogeneous difference equation with constant coefficients. Instead of pursuing the solution technique outlined earlier, we can, because of its simplicity, solve this difference equation using an iterative method. Let the initial condition, when $t = 0$ be $X_t = X_0$. For

82

$$t = 1 \quad \text{this gives} \quad X_1 - aX_0 = 0 \quad \text{or} \quad X_1 = aX_0$$
$$t = 2 \quad \text{this gives} \quad X_2 - aX_1 = 0 \quad \text{or} \quad X_2 = a^2X_0$$
$$t = 3 \quad \text{this gives} \quad X_3 - aX_2 = 0 \quad \text{or} \quad X_3 = a^3X_0$$

$$\vdots \qquad\qquad\qquad \vdots \qquad\qquad\qquad \vdots$$

$$t = n \quad \text{this gives} \quad X_n - aX_{n-1} = 0 \quad \text{or} \quad X_n = a^nX_0$$

From inspection it follows that the general solution for a first-order homogeneous difference equation is

$$X_t = a^t X_0, \tag{A.7}$$

where $t = 1, 2, \ldots, n$.

It will be left to the reader to check whether the solution satisfies the two requirements.

FIRST-ORDER NON-HOMOGENEOUS DIFFERENCE EQUATIONS

Let

$$X_t - aX_{t-1} - b = 0 \tag{A.8}$$

be a first-order non-homogeneous difference equation, with the initial condition $X_t = X_0$ when $t = 0$.

First the homogeneous solution is to be obtained. As a first step the additive constant b, will be set equal to zero. For the remaining homogeneous form

$$X_t - aX_{t-1} = 0 \tag{A.9}$$

we try as a possible solution $X_t = \lambda^t$. After substitution and dividing by λ^{t-1} we obtain: $\lambda - a = 0$. Hence, $\lambda = a$, which is the value for the root of the reduced equation.

The homogeneous solution is now

$$X_t = a^t A \tag{A.10}$$

where A the constant to be determined by the initial condition does *not*, as in the previous case, imply $A = X_0$.

Next the particular solution is obtained by setting

$$X_t = X_{t-1} = \bar{X}$$

83

and substituting this into equation (A.8),[1] thus

$$\bar{X} - a\bar{X} - b = 0$$

and

$$\bar{X} = b/(1-a). \tag{A.11}$$

The general solution is

$$X_t = a^t A + b/(1-a). \tag{A.12}$$

This form satisfies the difference equation, but not yet the initial values. To achieve this we proceed as follows. Let the initial value for X_t, at $t = 0$, be X_0. Substitution into equation (A.12) for $t = 0$

$$X_0 = A + b/(1-a) \quad \text{or} \quad A = X_0 - b/(1-a).$$

Substituting this result back into (A.12)

$$X_t = \left(X_0 - \frac{b}{a-1}\right)(a)^t + \frac{b}{1-a} \tag{A.13}$$

then gives the *definite* solution since it satisfies the given initial value of X. The solution can be interpreted as follows.

The set of constant coefficients, $b/(1-a)$, determines the trend or equilibrium value of X, $(\bar{X})$, since it was obtained by setting $X_t = X_{t-1}$. The time path of deviations around the equilibrium value, $X_t - \bar{X}$, is determined by the value of $(a)^t$, which is the only relevant coefficient for stability analysis, see Fig. 16. Examples of the various time paths are in Fig. 17.

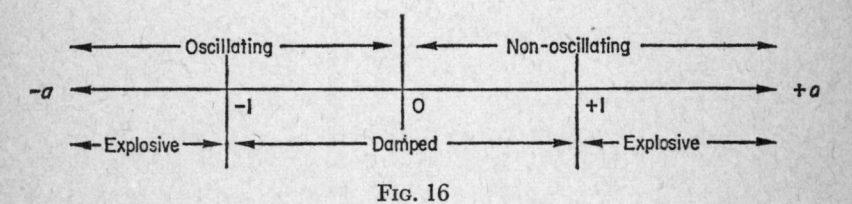

FIG. 16

[1] In some cases this may not work as in

$$X_t - 2X_{t-1} + X_{t-2} = 2$$

one should then try $X_t = \bar{X}t$ or $X_t = \bar{X}t^2$.

84

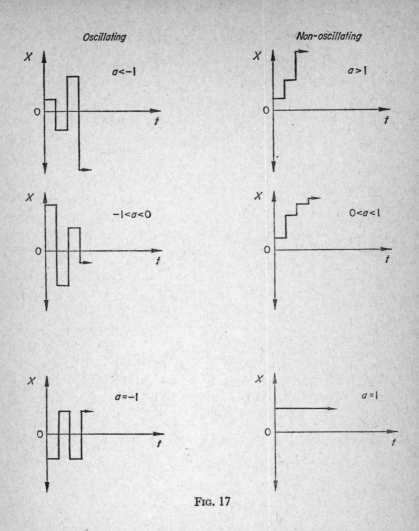

Fig. 17

SECOND-ORDER DIFFERENCE EQUATIONS

Let

$$X_t + a_1 X_{t-1} + a_2 X_{t-2} = f(t) \tag{A.14}$$

be a linear difference equation with constant coefficients. The order of the equation is $t - (t-2) = 2$. When $f(t)$ is a constant b, equation (A.14) is rewritten as

$$X_t + a_1 X_{t-1} + a_2 X_{t-2} - b = 0 \qquad (A.15)$$

To obtain the general solution we first try to find the particular one.

Let $X_t = X_{t-1} = X_{t-2} = \bar{X}$. Substitute into equation (A.15)

$$(1 + a_1 + a_2)\bar{X} = b \quad \text{or} \quad \bar{X} = \frac{b}{1 + a_1 + a_2} \qquad (A.16)$$

This represents the equilibrium value of X_t.

The homogeneous form of (A.15) is

$$X_t + a_1 X_{t-1} + a_2 X_{t-2} = 0 \qquad (A.17)$$

Substitute first $X_t = \lambda^t$ and then divide all terms by λ^{t-2}. The result is a quadratic auxiliary equation in λ,

$$\lambda^2 + a_1 \lambda + a_2 = 0 \qquad (A.18)$$

with two roots

$$\lambda_{1,2} = \frac{-a_1 \pm (a^2_1 - 4a_2)^{1/2}}{2}$$

Three possibilities have to be considered.

(1) $\qquad\qquad a^2_1 = 4a_2,$

where the roots are real and equal, that is $\lambda_1 = \lambda_2 = -\tfrac{1}{2}a_1$. The general solution becomes

$$X_t = \bar{X} + A_1(-\tfrac{1}{2}a_1)^t + A_2 t(-\tfrac{1}{2}a_1)^t \qquad (A.19)$$

a result of more mathematical interest than economic.

(2) $\qquad\qquad a^2_1 > 4a_2$

where the quantity under the radical is positive, and the roots of the auxiliary equation are real and different. The general solution is

$$X_t = \bar{X} + A_1(\lambda_1)^t + A_2(\lambda_2)^t \qquad (A.20)$$

For stability only the dominant root is of concern. If λ_1 is the dominant root, then λ_2 will not influence the solution as t gets larger but X_t will converge to $\bar{X}$ if $\lambda_1 < 1$ and will diverge if $\lambda_1 > 1$.

(3) $$a^2_1 < 4a_2$$

This implies a negative quantity under the radical, and subsequently the roots will be complex numbers. To analyse this case a new number will have to be defined, which accounts for negative quantities under the radical. Thus we define $i = (-1)^{1/2}$. The roots of the auxiliary equation are now rewritten as

$$\lambda_1 = -\tfrac{1}{2}a_1 + i(a_2 - \tfrac{1}{4}a^2_1)^{1/2} \tag{A.21}$$

and

$$\lambda_2 = -\tfrac{1}{2}a_1 - i(a_2 - \tfrac{1}{4}a^2_1)^{1/2} \tag{A.22}$$

where λ_1 and λ_2 are called conjugate complex numbers.

It is convenient to use a diagram to illustrate the analysis, measuring i, on the vertical axis and real numbers on the horizontal one as in Fig. 18 (p.88), where $OQ = -\tfrac{1}{2}a_1$, $PQ = (a_2 - \tfrac{1}{4}a^2_1)^{1/2}$, and $RQ = (a_2 - \tfrac{1}{4}a^2_1)^{1/2}$. Root λ_1 is determined by the distance OP and the angle θ, and root λ_2 by OR and $-\theta$. We are looking for a solution that reflects both factors.

A Pythagoras theorem states

$$OP = \{(OQ)^2 + (PQ)^2\}^{1/2}$$

in our case

$$OP = \{(-\tfrac{1}{2}a_1)^2 + a_2 - \tfrac{1}{4}a^2_1\}^{1/2} = a_2$$

and the same result applies for OR. Further

$$PQ = OP \sin \theta \qquad (\sin \theta = PQ/OP)$$

and

$$OQ = OP \cos \theta \qquad (\cos \theta = OQ/OP).$$

Since $\lambda_1 = iPQ + OQ$ and $\lambda_2 = -iPQ + OQ$ we can express the value of the roots in trigonometric notation:

$$\begin{aligned} \lambda_1 &= iOP \sin \theta + OP \cos \theta \\ &= a_2(i \sin \theta + \cos \theta) \end{aligned} \tag{A.23}$$

and

$$\lambda_2 = a_2(\cos \theta - i \sin \theta) \tag{A.24}$$

The general solution is now

$$X_t = \bar{X} + A_1(a_2)^t(\cos \theta + i \sin \theta)^t + A_2(a_2)^t(\cos \theta - i \sin \theta)^t. \tag{A.25}$$

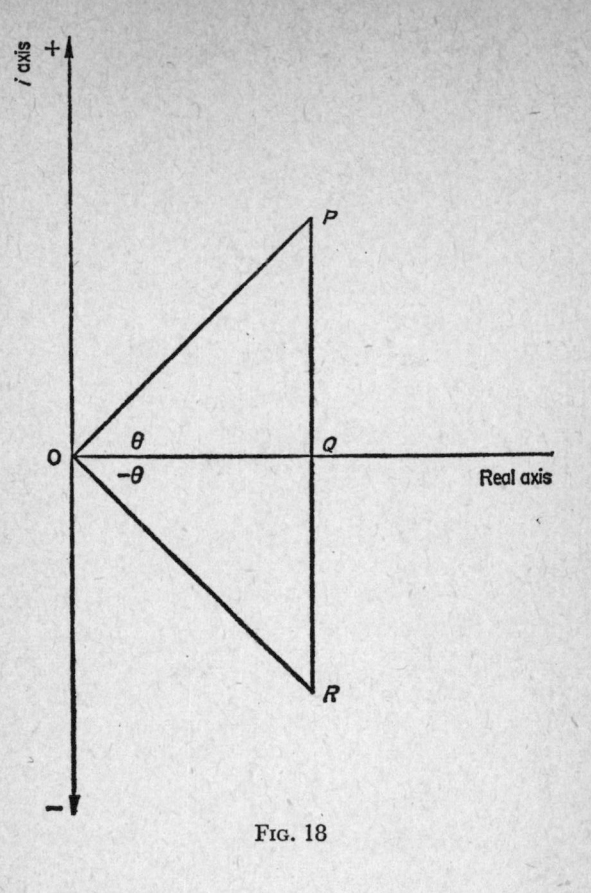

FIG. 18

By De Moivre's theorem

$$(\cos \theta \pm \sin \theta)^t = \cos t\,\theta \pm \sin t\,\theta. \qquad (A.26)$$

The general situation is then simplified to,

$$X_t = \bar{X} + a^t{}_2\{(A_1 + A_2)\cos t\theta + (A_1 - A_2)i\sin t\theta\} \qquad (A.27)$$

Sine and cosine functions describe a periodic movement. The general solution will therefore oscillate. It will be stable if $a_2 < 1$, and explosive if $a_2 > 1$. Oscillations of uniform amplitude occur when $a_2 = 1$.

The results of the interpretation of the solution of second-order difference equations is neatly summarised in Fig. 19. The field of relevant values for a_1 and a_2 is divided into several regions in the following way.

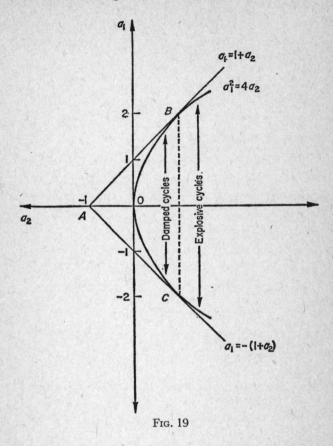

Fig. 19

The region with combinations of values for a_1 and a_2, representing real roots in the auxiliary equation, is bounded from the complex roots region by the parabola $a^2_1 = 4a_2$ (corresponding with zero values under the radical). The value for a_2 determines the (in)stability of a *cyclical* system, hence, a perpendicular through a_2 divides the complex roots region into a stable part where $a_2 < 1$, and an unstable part where $a_2 > 1$. So far three regions are defined: one outside the parabola where the roots are real and different and two inside. But within the first region a few more subregions can be distinguished.

For stability in the real roots case, it is required for the dominant root to be $|\lambda_1| < 1$. There are two possibilities:

(1) when $0 < \lambda_1 < 1$, and
(2) when $-1 < \lambda_1 < 0$.

In the first case, the stability condition can be rewritten as

$$0 < (1 - \lambda_1)(1 - \lambda_2) \tag{A.28}$$

substituting values for λ_1 and λ_2

$$0 < 1 + a_1 + a_2$$

or

$$a_1 > -(1 + a_2) \tag{A.29}$$

By drawing $a_1 = -(1 + a_2)$, two more regions can now be distinguished: a region at the left-hand side of the line, representing unstable combinations, and a region at the right-hand side of the line, representing stable combinations.

In the second case, the stability condition $-1 < \lambda_1 < 0$ is rewritten as

$$0 < (1 + \lambda_1)(1 + \lambda_2) \tag{A.30}$$

again substituting values for λ_1 and λ_2 results as:

$$a_1 < 1 + a_2 \tag{A.31}$$

Graphing $a_1 = 1 + a_2$, again produces two regions, one at the left-hand side of the line through $a_2 = -1$ and $a_1 = +1$ representing unstable solutions, the region at the other side representing stable solutions. Since the dominant root is negative, both solutions, the stable and the unstable, will show an alternating time path not a monotonic one. All stable solutions, whether monotonic or alternating or cyclical are found in the triangle ABC.

Bibliography

[1] A. A. Alchian, 'Information Costs, Pricing and Resource Employment', *Western Economic Journal* (June 1969). Reprinted in E. S. Phelps, *et al.*, *Microeconomic Foundations of Employment and Inflation Theory* (Norton, New York, 1970).

[2] R. G. D. Allen, *Macro-Economic Theory* (Macmillan, London, 1967).

[3] S. Almon, 'The Distributed Lag between Capital Appropriations and Expenditures', *Econometrica* (January 1965).

[4] K. J. Arrow and M. Nerlove, 'A Note on Expectations and Stability', *Econometrica* (April 1958).

[5] K. J. Arrow and W. M. Capron, 'Dynamic Shortages and Price Rises: The Engineer–Scientist Case', *Quarterly Journal of Economics* (April 1959). Reprinted in M. Blaug, *Economics of Education*, ı (Penguin, Harmondsworth, 1968).

[6] W. J. Baumol, 'Pitfalls in Contracyclical Policies: Some Tools and Results', *Review of Economics and Statistics* (February 1961).

[7] W. J. Baumol, *Economic Dynamics* (Collier-Macmillan, New York, 1970).

[8] T. M. Brown, 'Habit Persistence and Lags in Consumer Behavior', *Econometrica* (July 1952).

[9] D. W. Bushaw and R. W. Clower, *Introduction to Mathematical Economics* (R. D. Irwin, Homewood, Ill., 1957).

[10] P. Cagan, 'The Monetary Dynamics of Hyperinflation', in *Studies in the Quantity Theory of Money* (Aldine, Chicago, 1956).

[11] A. Cairncross (ed.), *Britain's Economic Prospects Reconsidered* (Allen & Unwin, London, 1971).

[12] John A. Carlson, 'The Production Lag', *American Economic Review* (January 1973).

[13] R. A. Caves (ed.), *Britain's Economic Prospects* (Allen & Unwin, London, 1968).

[14] R. W. Clower, 'The Keynesian Counter-Revolution: A Theoretical Appraisal', in *The Theory of Interest Rates*, ed. F. H. Hahn and F. Brechling (Macmillan, London, 1965).

[15] A. D. Crockett, 'Timing Relationships between Movements of Monetary and National Income Variables', *Bank of England Quarterly Bulletin* (December 1970).

[16] F. De Leeuw, 'The Demand for Capital Goods by Manufacturers: A Study of Quarterly Time Series', *Econometrica* (July 1962).

[17] E. A. Devletoglou, 'Correct Public Prediction and the Stability of Equilibrium', *Journal of Political Economy* (April 1961).

[18] J. R. C. Dow, *The Management of the British Economy* (N.I.E.S.R. and Cambridge University Press, London, 1964).

[19] J. S. Duesenberry, *Income, Saving, and the Theory of Consumer Behavior* (Harvard University Press, 1949).

[20] M. K. Evans, *Macro-Economic Activity* (Harper & Row, New York, 1969).

[21] M. Friedman, 'The Effects of a Full-Employment Policy on Economic Stability; A Formal Analysis', in *Essays in Positive Economics* (University of Chicago Press, 1953).

[22] M. Friedman, *A Theory of the Consumption Function* (Princeton University Press, 1957).

[23] M. Friedman and A. J. Schwartz, 'Money and Business Cycles', *Review of Economics and Statistics* (February 1963).

[24] M. Friedman, *The Optimum Quantity of Money* (Aldine, Chicago, 1969).

[25] M. Friedman, 'Have Monetary Policies Failed?', *American Economic Review* (May 1972).

[26] R. Frisch, 'Propagation Problems and Impulse Problems in Dynamic Economics', in *Economic Essays in Honour of Gustav Cassel* (Allen & Unwin, London, 1933).

[27] R. Frisch, 'On the Notion of Equilibrium and Disequilibrium', *Review of Economic Studies*, III (1935–6).

[28] R. M. Goodwin, 'Dynamical Coupling with Especial Reference to Markets having Production Lags', *Econometrica* (July 1947).

[29] R. M. Goodwin, 'Iteration, Automatic Computers and Economic Dynamics', *Metroeconomica* (April 1951).

[30] Z. Griliches, 'Distributed Lags: A Survey', *Econometrica* (January 1967).

[31] E. Grunberg and F. Modigliani, 'The Predictability of Social Events', *Journal of Political Economy* (December 1954).

[32] F. H. Hahn and R. C. O. Matthews, 'The Theory ~ ~ Economic Growth: A Survey', in *Surveys of Economic Theory*, vol. H (Macmillan, London, 1967).

[33] A. Hanau, 'Die Prognose der Schweinepreise', *Vierteljahrshefte zur Konjunkturforschung* (Sonderheft 18, Berlin, 1930).

[34] J. M. Henderson and R. E. Quandt, *Microeconomic Theory* (McGraw-Hill, New York, 1958).

[35] J. D. Hey, 'Price Adjustment in an Atomistic Market', *Journal of Economic Theory* (August 1974).

[36] J. R. Hicks, *Value and Capital* (Oxford University Press, 1939).

[37] J. R. Hicks, *A Contribution to the Theory of the Trade Cycle* (Oxford University Press, 1950).

[38] J. R. Hicks, *Capital and Growth* (Oxford University Press, 1965).

[39] A. G. Hines, *On the Reappraisal of Keynesian Economics* (Martin Robertson, London, 1970).

[40] W. A. B. Hopkin and W. A. H. Godley, 'An Analysis of Tax Changes', *National Institute Economic Review* (May 1965).

[41] O. B. Jesness, 'Changes in the Agricultural Adjustment Program in the Past 25 Years', *Journal of Farm Economics* (May 1958).

[42] D. W. Jorgenson, 'Rational Distributed Lag Functions', *Econometrica* (January 1966).

[43] P. N. Junankar, *Investment: Theories and Evidence* (Macmillan, London, 1972).

[44] M. Kalecki, 'A Macro-dynamic Theory of Business Cycles', *Econometrica*, vol. 3 (1935).

[45] L. R. Klein, 'The Treatment of Expectations in Econometrics', in *Uncertainty and Expectations in Economics, Essays in Honour of G. L. S. Shackle*, ed. C. F. Carter and J. L. Ford (Basil Blackwell, Oxford, 1972).

[46] L. M. Koyck, *Distributed Lags and Investment Analysis* (North-Holland, Amsterdam, 1954).

[47] A. Leijonhufvud, *On Keynesian Economics and the Economics of Keynes* (Oxford University Press, 1968).

[48] A. Leijonhufvud, *Keynes and the Classics*, Institute of Economics Affairs Occasional Paper 30 (1969).

[49] E. Lundberg, *Studies in the Theory of Economic Expansion* (P. S. King, London, 1937).

[50] F. Machlup, 'Equilibrium and Disequilibrium', *The Economic Journal* (March 1958). Reprinted in *Essays on Economic Semantics* (Prentice-Hall, Englewood Cliffs, N.J., 1963).

[51] F. Machlup, 'Statics and Dynamics', *The Southern Economic Journal* (October 1959). Reprinted in the same author's *Essays on Economic Semantics* (Prentice-Hall, Englewood Cliffs, N.J., 1963).

[52] Lloyd A. Metzler, 'The Nature and Stability of Inventory Cycles', *Review of Economics and Statistics* (August 1941).

[53] Lloyd A. Metzler, 'Three Lags in the Circular Flow of Income', in *Income Employment and Public Policy: Essays in Honour of Alvin H. Hansen* (Norton, New York, 1948).

[54] F. Modigliani, 'Fluctuations in the Saving – Income Ratio: A Problem in Economic Forecasting', in *Studies in Income and Wealth*, vol. ii (New York, 1949).

[55] R. A. Musgrave, *The Theory of Public Finance* (McGraw-Hill, New York, 1959).

[56] J. F. Muth, 'Rational Expectations and the Theory of Price Movements', *Econometrica* (July 1961).

[57] M. Nerlove, 'Adaptive Expectations and Cobweb Phenomena', *Quarterly Journal of Economics* (May 1958).

[58] M. Nerlove, 'Lags in Economic Behaviour', *Econometrica* (March 1972).

[59] A. W. Phillips, 'Stabilisation Policy in a Closed Economy', *Economic Journal* (June 1954).

[60] A. W. Phillips, 'Stabilisation Policy and the Time-Forms of Lagged Responses', *Economic Journal* (June 1957).

[61] R. H. Rasche and H. T. Shapiro, 'The F.R.B.–M.I.T. Econometric Model: Its Special Features', *American Economic Review* (May 1968).

[62] N. Rau, *Trade Cycles: Theory and Evidence* (Macmillan, London, 1974).

[63] D. H. Robertson, 'Some Notes on Mr. Keynes' General Theory of Employment', *Quarterly Journal of Economics*, vol. LI (1937).

[64] M. Rothschild, 'Models of Market Organisation with Imperfect Information: A Survey', *Journal of Political Economy* (November/December 1973).

[65] P. A. Samuelson, 'Interactions Between the Multiplier Analysis and the Principle of Acceleration', *Review of Economics and Statistics* (May 1939).

[66] P. A. Samuelson, *Foundations of Economic Analysis* (Harvard University Press, 1947).

[67] J. R. Shephard and M. J. C. Surrey, 'The Short-Term Effects of Tax Changes', *National Institute Economic Review* (November 1968).

[68] H. A. Simon, 'Application of Servomechanism Theory to Production Control', in the same author's *Models of Man* (Wiley, New York, 1957).

[69] R. M. Solow, 'On a Family of Lag Distributions', *Econometrica* (April 1960).

[70] R. M. Solow, *Price Expectations and the Behavior of the Price Level* (Manchester University Press, 1969).

[71] G. J. Stigler, 'The Economics of Information', *Journal of Political Economy* (June 1961).

[72] G. J. Stigler, 'Information in the Labor Market', *Journal of Political Economy* (October 1962).

[73] D. B. Suits and S. Koizumi, 'The Dynamics of the Onion Market', *Journal of Farm Economics* (May 1956).

[74] M. J. C. Surrey, *The Analysis and Forecasting of The British Economy* (N.I.E.S.R. and Cambridge University Press, 1971).

[75] J. Tinbergen, 'Bestimmung und Deutung von Angebots-kurven. Ein Beispiel', *Zeitschrift für Nationalökonomie*, I, Heft 5 (April 1930).

[76] J. Tinbergen, 'Annual Survey: Suggestions on Quantitative Business Cycle Theory', *Econometrica*, III (1935).

[77] J. Tinbergen, 'An Economic Policy for 1936', reprinted in *Jan Tinbergen: Selected Papers* (North-Holland, Amsterdam, 1959).

[78] J. Tinbergen, 'Lag Cycles and Life Cycles', reprinted in *Jan Tinbergen: Selected Papers* (North-Holland, Amsterdam, 1959).

[79] K. F. Wallis, 'Some Recent Developments in Applied Econometrics', *Journal of Economic Literature* (September 1969).

[80] A. A. Walters, 'Monetary Multipliers in the United Kingdom', *Oxford Economic Papers* (November 1966).